Learn How to Harness the Power of Rune Might!

Rune Might reveals, for the first time in the English language, the long-hidden secrets of the German rune magicians who practiced their arts in the beginning of this century. Most of their work has been unavailable even in German for several decades.

By studying the contents of *Rune Might* and working with the exercises, you will be introduced to a fascinating world of magical personalities and the sometimes sinister dark corners of runic history. Beyond this, the reader will be able to experience the direct power of the runes as experienced by the early German rune magicians.

Rune Might takes the best and most powerful of the runic techniques developed in that early phase of the runic revival and offers them as a coherent set of exercises. Experience rune yoga, rune dance, runic hand gestures (mudras), rune singing (mantras), group rites with runes, runic healing, and two of the most powerful runic methods of engaging transpersonal powers—the Ritual of the Ninth Night and the Ritual of the Graal-Cup.

The exercises represent bold new methods of drawing magical power into your life—regardless of the magical tradition or system with which you normally work. Rune exercises can be incorporated into any magical curriculum. The runes can be used to focus various qualities of magical force—as absorbed from the Earth, the atmosphere, or the outer reaches of the cosmos—in the personal sphere of the magician. No other system does this in quite the direct and clearly defined ways that rune exercises do.

For those who have recently rediscovered the magic of the runes, this book provides a useful supplement. The magical heritage of the runes will become clearer to those who experience their power through the formulae that gave the first magical impulse to the runic revival.

Llewellyn's Teutonic Magick Series

Teutonic Magick is as vast as the northern sky and as deep as the shrouded northern mists.

Many of the most powerful forms of magick in the West were developed to an early perfection by Teutonic magicians—Albertus Magnus, Agrippa, Paracelsus—some were even elevated to the level of legend, such as Faustus.

Teutonic magick is multifaceted—it has its own innate traditions—those of the ancient Germanic peoples (Anglo-Saxons, Germans, Dutch, Scandinavians) and in addition it has those of the general Western Tradition, which they received from southern Europe in the Middle Ages—and proceeded to develop with characteristic scientific zeal.

The world of Teutonic Magick is full of truly secret, some sinister, corners as well. Many of these—like so much else that we believe to be sinister—are thus characterized simply because unknown and perhaps also misunderstood. There are whole realms of Teutonic magick that have largely been kept truly secret until the latter part of this century.

Llewellyn's Teutonic Magick Series is the first to explore this world in a systematic and authoritative way. It will reveal the secrets of German rune magic, the obscure mysteries of Gothic Kabbalah, the magic of Faustus, and the deepest mysteries of the German occult orders such as the Rosicrucians, the Illuminati, the Fraternitas Saturni, and the dreaded FOGC-Lodge.

The path of Teutonic Magick is focused on the expansion of consciousness through a will to power and knowledge—the way opened for the Teutonic magician by Woden on an archetypal level and followed by Faustus and most modern magicians.

Other books by Edred Thorsson

Futhark: A Handbook of Rune Magic
Runelore: A Handbook of Esoteric Runology
At the Well of Wyrd: A Handbook of Runic Divination
A Book of Troth
Fire and Ice
The Nine Doors of Midgard
The Book of Ogham
Northern Magic

Llewellyn's Teutonic Magick Series

Rune Might

Secret Practices of the German Rune Magicians

Edred Thorsson

1994
Llewellyn Publications
St. Paul, Minnesota 55164-0383, U.S.A.

FIRST EDITION
Third Printing, 1994

Cover painting by Lissanne Lake

Library of Congress Cataloging-in-Publication Data
Thorsson, Edred.
    Rune might: secret practices of the German rune magicians / by
Edred Thorsson.
        p.   cm. — (Llewellyn's Teutonic magick series)
    Includes bibliographical references.
    ISBN 0-87542-778-2
    1. Runes—Miscellanea. 2. Magic, Germanic. I. Title. II. Series.
BF1623.R89T485   1989
133.4'3—dc20   89-35506
                                                            CIP

133.43
Tho

Llewellyn Publications
A Division of Llewellyn Worldwide, Ltd.
P.O. Box 64383, St. Paul, MN 55164-0383

To the Trailblazers

Contents

Figures

Tables

List of Abbreviations

B.C.E.   Before the Common Era (B.C.)

C.E.   Common Era (A.D.)

G.   German

Preface

Since the middle of the 1970s there has been a significant renaissance in the study and practice of the runes in Anglo-American occult circles. This has been an unusual aspect of the occult revival in these circles, but in Germany the runes have been a general part of the occult revival almost from its beginning in the late nineteenth century. The degree to which the traditions of rune magic form a distinct and coherent part of the general Western tradition is unclear. This is because this tradition has been practiced completely outside the realm of modern English-speaking magicians until quite recently. Given that the runes have been widely used and explored in German occult circles, it seems that those persons in the English-speaking world interested in working with the runes may have a thing or two to learn from the German tradition of rune work.

To a large extent the German rune magicians of the early part of this century were eclectics. They gathered magical practices from various better-known systems and "runicized" them. Because of the traditions (and in many cases nontraditions) that the Anglo-American runic revival have often followed, the Armanic system (18-rune futhork) generally used by the German rune magicians will have some drawbacks. But what I intend to explore in this book are the practical techniques pioneered by the German rune magicians.

For those who are fairly well immersed in another magical system, the runic techniques contained in this book can offer some new ideas to vivify the system with which you are familiar. For those who take an eclectic and perhaps pragmatic approach to magic, the runic techniques you will find here are ideal experimental material for the expansion of your magical repertoire. For those already engaged in serious, traditional rune work (for example, with the Rune-Gild), this book will give some in-depth, practical insight into the dawn of the magical runic revival and will help put your work into a larger historical framework.

There have been a number of books about rune magic produced over the past several years. Some have been good, although most have been fairly poor. But no book published in English has yet undertaken to explain the practical aspects of the rune magic practiced in twentieth-century occult circles. It is a complex and rich magical heritage, and here we will only be able to begin to open the door to this world.

Introduction

Magical practice dealing with runes and the use of runic lore to shape occult teachings has a long history in Germany. For almost as long as there has been a magical revival in that country, there has been a magical runic revival. In the annals of this renaissance, two names shine out above all the rest: Guido von List and Friedrich Bernhard Marby. Others would expand and adapt their ideas, but without doubt all of the significant magical innovations of the occult German runic revival can be traced to one or the other of these two men. But in this work we will be dealing not only with the secret teachings of these two but also with that of their followers and students, each of whom added something to the hoard of teachings that make up the German occult tradition surrounding the runes.

In the present work I want to explore the practical teachings and workings of the German rune magicians. It will be shown how the German runic tradition fits nicely with the Western magical tradition, for it is an outgrowth of it, although the rune magician would argue that it is the deepest root and basis of the Western revival itself. The second part of this book is a collection of some of the most influential and powerful workings of the German rune-magic tradition. The techniques are drawn from a wide range of books, mostly printed in the 1920s, 1930s, and 1950s. They represent the secret teachings of various esoteric groups working with the runes in Germany during the early part of this century. The reader will be able to enact these runic workings and exercises for purposes of self-development, strengthening the will, and generally improving all phases of magical work. The runes, as taught in the Armanic system, can very easily be put into the working context of any other Western magical tradition, in contrast to the highly traditional forms of runelore expressed in the 24-rune futhark, which is fairly intolerant of admixture with other systems. This is simply because the 18-rune futhork as used by the Armanen (the followers of Guido von List) and most other German rune magicians of this time is more a part of the Western tradition than is the 24-rune system. If one is going to work "eclectically" with the runes, it is perhaps best to work with the Armanic runes (the 18-rune futhork).

Part I

Background

Chapter 1

Early History

A rune is a *mystery* first and foremost. It is only later that the term is used to designate a letter or writing symbol. In ancient times the term was most likely used to designate a variety of signs and symbols, of which only a certain codified group became the runestaves employed in writing natural language.

In the German tradition, mystical theories about how and when the runes originated and what their usages were in prehistoric times are at great variance with the theories of academic scholars. The esoteric runologists of early twentieth-century Germany generally held ideas that kept them forever at odds with the available scientific data produced by exoteric, or academic, runologists. There is indeed that place and that key which opens the door between these two worlds, and these two views, about the runes. But it can only be found through actual initiation into the mysteries themselves.

The academic runologists generally declare that the runes and the notion of writing itself was borrowed in a unique and original form by the ancient Teutonic peoples sometime between 300 and 100 B.C.E. The original runic system is considered the Elder Futhark of 24 runestaves, expanded by the Anglo-Frisians to as many as 33 runestaves, and reduced by the Viking Age Scandinavians to 16. Originally these signs had their own unique order and had traditional names associated with various aspects of the spiritual lore of the Teutonic folk. (See chapter 6 for further information on the ancient runic traditions.) Eventually the runic tradition was obscured as the system of the Roman alphabet grew in importance during the Middle Ages, and finally it was lost altogether.

Although there are a variety of traditions in German occult circles regarding the origins of the runes, most agree on two things: that the runes are essentially cosmic encodements in the very beings of the Teutonic folk, and that they were originally formulated within a vastly ancient— perhaps antediluvian—civilization. This primeval culture is generally associated with Atlantis (Atland), Thule, Mother-Land, or Hyperborea, and in all cases placed in the North.

Guido von List and his followers found much in the esoteric teachings of Theosophy corroborating their findings—that the Aryans* were essentially Nordics of a high level of spiritual and material culture who came from the northern regions to civilize the world. Wherever they went they took the runes and the other holy signs of their people. These signs were the physical expression of the inner mysteries of the world that were obvious and fully conscious to the ancient Aryans. These mysteries, and hence the runes, became obscured as they mixed with and were diluted by peoples and traditions other than their own.

The chief mission of the runes, in the view of many of the German rune magicians, is to help reawaken this

*List and other writers of this period, following the lead of both academics and Theosophists, referred to the group of people we now call Indo-European with this somewhat antiquated and slightly tainted word.

ability and this vital essence lost in times past. The runes are the mysteries and the key to the mysteries at the same time. They have existed eternally within the folk-soul of the Teutons and await only their full reawakening.

List claims that the 18-rune futhork is the original form of the runic system and that all others are derived from it by adding extra symbols.

According to Friedrich Bernhard Marby, the runes originated in the Mother-Land, which sank below the waves of the North Sea some 12,000 years ago. For Marby it was the 33-rune Anglo-Frisian Futhorc that came closest to the original form of the rune-row, although he thought that the original system must have contained even more signs.

The esoteric German traditions concerning the history of Teutonic religion and magic (especially that of the runes) are based very much on the idea that the ancient ways were taken underground into the structure, myth, and ritual of the medieval Christian Church. At first these concealments were quite intentional and conscious on the part of Armanen. These Armanen, or priests, "converted" to Catholicism and infused their religious symbolism and wisdom into that of the Church. But with time the keys to the hidden meanings of the original Armanic customs and practices were lost. However, the forms remained, and it is these forms that can now be unlocked with the knowledge provided by the runes and by the remanifestation of the Teutonic folk-soul.

Long before the Runic Spring of the early part of this century, there was an earlier flowering of an esoteric runic tradition. This was essentially the work of the much neglected Swedish scholar and mystic, Johannes Bureus (ᛉ 1568– ᛣ 1652). Bureus was one of the first scholarly runologists, who collected many runic texts from Swedish runestones and began to interpret them in a well-informed manner. He also had a mystical side. Bureus was a Paracelsist, well versed in the lore of the Kabbalah and the magical techniques of Agrippa von Nettesheim. This was also the age of *storgoticism*—Great-Gothicism—the esoteric doctrine that the Goths (wrongly assumed to be the same as the Swedes) were the once and future master race. Bureus had become the "high priest" of this movement from his chair at the University of Uppsala. To Bureus the runes were the primeval script containing great mysteries that could be read from an initiated perspective. This he did through a system he called "adulrunes," which was a variation on the Kabbalistic method known as *temura*.

German rune magic was revived not in the tradition of Johannes Bureus but through a synthesis of the school of German Romanticism and the occult revival of the late nineteenth and early twentieth century.

Throughout the 1800s there was a growing interest in the ancient traditions of the North. This was in large part a reflection of the Romantic (some might call it "Germantic" or "Gothick") urge to turn inward, into the depths of the self, in a quest for ultimate reality. In a way, this urge in the individual was reflected in the next higher organic unity— the nation, or folk. Thus the folk began to turn inward and seek within their own traditions and lore for that which they had formerly looked in vain outside themselves. Christianity and the traditions of the South had been found wanting—the truth was to be found within.

The traditional knowledge, as preserved within the folk itself, was quite decayed by this time. Centuries of ignorance and lack of training had left what remained of the folk traditions rather empty. The only possible exception to this would be the preservation of the family traditions of the German "occult nobility," supposedly as represented by such claimants as Tarnhari (E. Lauterer) and Lobesam (K. M. Wiligut). These men claimed to be the repositories of ancient initiatory family traditions, and if this is true they would be remarkable examples of how the ancient traditions were handed down along family lines. Similar traditions were, of course, often found among early revivers of the Wiccan way in England.

It was more usual, however, for men such as Guido von List to claim extraordinary powers of insight and vision, which enabled them to reconstruct the past through a combination of clairvoyance and research in the folk ways and customs.

The late nineteenth century saw the coming of the occult revival to Germany. German-speaking central Europe (Germany, Austria, Switzerland, etc.) had long been a breeding ground for esoteric and magical schools. Agrippa, Paracelsus, Boehme, and Albertus Magnus had all been Germans, and the schools of Rosicrucianism and Illuminism had originated there. So the occult was certainly no stranger to the land when it bloomed forth in the 1880s and 1890s, largely as a byproduct of the introduction of Theosophy to the region. This brought out into the open what had been much more secret up to that time. The magical and the esoteric became something that could be openly espoused and promoted, and thus the foundations were laid for the Runic Spring.

Chapter 2

The Armanic Renaissance
(1904–1919)

T he bloom of the Runic Spring lasted from about 1904, when the Guido von List Society was founded, to the beginning of the First World War in 1914. This conflict brought the Spring to a stormy end and heralded even more disastrous times to come. But the runes are no strangers to strife.

Above all others, the figure of Guido von List (ᛀ October 5, 1848, Vienna– ᛣ May 17, 1919, Berlin) looms over the history of the revival of runic occultism. It is to List that almost all of the subsequent rune-magic works and runic esoterica trace their origins. List was the son of a wealthy Viennese businessman, but instead of following in his father's footsteps he turned his attentions first to the writing of journalism, then to novels and dramas, and finally, in the last 15 years of his life, to esoteric studies. It is important to understand that List never published anything of a practical magical nature. He was more the visionary of the movement. But he was in many ways a magician, and many of his insights were used in practical ways. (See, for example, the use of his linguistic theories in the construction of mantras in chapter 8.) It is obvious that he wanted to keep the practical teachings of rune magic secret. The details of List's life and ideas can be found in Stephen Flowers' translation and study of *The Secret of the Runes*, List's seminal work.

In *The Secret of the Runes* (1908) List reveals his theory that the original rune-row was an 18-rune futhork (otherwise unknown in the annals of runology). This system is based on the "scriptural" evidence of the "Rúnatáls tháttr Odhins"—the last 28 stanzas of the "Hávamál" found in the *Poetic Edda*. List then went on to write several more books outlining many facets of the esoteric culture and religion of the ancient Teutons, or Aryo-Germanic peoples. List's methods of research were largely mysto-magical. He would gain visions of the ancient ways and then corroborate them through more conventional methods. Apparently some of his secret methods involved the raising of long-dead ancestral spirits to gain their wisdom. List's researches were supported by several wealthy industrialists. A Guido von List Society was founded to publish the Master's works and to support him financially. Members of this group included some of the leading figures from political, industrial, as well as occult, circles. Within this group there was a more esoteric inner cell called the Armanen Orden. Although this group never had a formal structure before List's death, it was the root of many runic developments to come.

List's visions and constructs were so compelling and his personality so dominant that his mystical system has been the rule in German runic occultism to this day. The only significantly independent voice in runic occultism was that of Friedrich Bernhard Marby.

Among List's students, one of the most influential was Philipp Stauff (ᚤ March 26, 1876, Moosbach– ᛉ July 17, 1923, Berlin), who joined the Guido von List Society in 1910. Stauff was an anti-Semitic journalist active in a number of nationalist organizations in Germany. In 1912 he moved to Berlin, and in that same year, published his greatest contribution to the history of runic esoterica, his book *Runenhäuser*. In this book Stauff theorized that the patterns made by the wooden beams in the half-timbered (*Fachwerk*) houses had a runic significance, and that one who knew the code could actually read the hidden meaning of the "rune-houses." This would later become a very popular aspect of esoteric runology. After List's death, it was Stauff who became president of the Society and continued to publish the works of the Master from the new headquarters in Berlin.

One of the most curious chapters of this phase of the runic revival was written by a man at first known only by the magical name "Tarnhari." In the Listian code language this name essentially meant "the hidden lord." Tarnhari sent a letter to List in November of 1911 in which he claimed to be the descendant/reincarnation of the head of the ancient Wölsung clan. In this letter Tarnhari revealed that his family traditions, which had been handed down from time immemorial, essentially corroborated all of List's clairvoyant researches into Germanic prehistory. It is interesting that Karl Maria Wiligut would make similar claims of "occult kingship" as well. Tarnhari, who was in actuality a man by the name of Ernst Lauterer, was very active in *völkisch* political organizations and was even a part of the post-World War I circle around Dietrich Eckart, the man who was Hitler's mentor and to whom Hitler dedicated *Mein Kampf*.

Among the many esoteric and political groups that promoted what they thought to be Germanic ideals, perhaps the one most involved with runic practices was the Germanen-Orden (Germanic Order), founded in 1912 by Hermann Pohl. In 1916 Pohl broke away from the order he had founded and set up an independent Germanen-Orden Walvater, which published the periodical *Runen* (Runes).

Runen contained many articles on runelore, and even some of an informative nature on rune magic. The Order also made talismanic bronze rings inscribed with magical runes available to its initiates. An illustration of one of these rings as it appeared in a 1919 issue of *Runen* is seen in Figure 2.1.

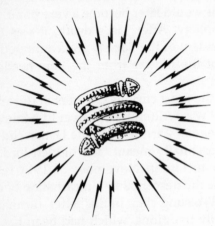

Figure 2.1 Runic Ring Advertised in *Runen*

The fundamental magical and mystical ideas promulgated in the Germanen-Orden were based on the system of Guido von List, coupled with the pseudoscientific racism of the day. It was from within the ranks of the Germanen-Orden that the famous Thule Society was formed in 1918 as a cover for the inner workings of the deeply mystical and political GO itself. The main center of activity for the Thule Society was Munich, and the main force behind it was the personality of Rudolf von Sebottendorf, who had traveled in various dark corners of the world collecting arcane lore.

To have any sort of true perspective on this time and place in history, one must realize that Germany and Austria had just been plunged into internal chaos by their political and economic defeat in the Great War, and that the whole region continued to be under overt attack by Communist revolutionary forces. Bavaria itself was under Communist rule for a few months in 1918–19, and was for a while even declared a Soviet republic. The Communists knew well that the Thule Society was an important cell of Nationalist resistance, and even took hostages from the Society and executed them. Again, to put this in perspective, the Communists were not only a threat, they had actually seized power; they did not only give lip service to "internationalism" (i.e., the obliteration of nationalities), they practiced it in that the revolution was being run by Russians. (This was long before Mr. Gorbachev discovered that nationalities cannot be destroyed but must be encouraged.) The worst nightmares of those who had dreamed of a Pan-Germanic culture had evaporated. All of this simply radicalized and more deeply politicized the groups involved in the restoration of the national traditions of their folk.

Chapter 3

The High Tide of Rune Magic
(1919-1935)

T he years following the death of Guido von List
and the end of the First World War were a time
of great expansion and dissemination with
regard to runic practices. The old groups were continuing,
but new ones were also springing up, and many began to
make the practical aspects of runelore more available. It is
not entirely incorrect to say that the spiritual, economic,
cultural, and political upheavals following the war encouraged this increased popularity of mystical and magical
thinking; but it would be wrong to assume that it caused
this interest. The runes and rune magic and mysticism have
their roots in the Germanic Spring, in a time when the
dream of national renewal based on self-determined values
was fully alive and highly optimistic. The cultural disap-
pointments brought on by the unhappy conclusion to the
Great War only put a bitter edge on the continuing movement and tended to spur it on not so much with the former
thoughts of an exuberance that wells up from within as with
the desire to strike out and avenge itself on those who it perceived to be the destroyers of the ancient dreams.

Rudolf John Gorsleben (ᛣ March 16, 1883, Metz–

ᚼ August 23, 1930, Bad Homburg) created a synthesis of the work and theories of Guido von List and the other rune occultists, Ariosophists, and Theosophists of the age. This synthesis is represented in his magnum opus, published in the year of his death, *Die Hoch-Zeit der Menschheit* (The Zenith [or High Tide] of Mankind). This work encompasses almost 700 pages and covers all of the major theoretical fields of neo-Germanic occultism popular at the time. But in it he avoids any practical instruction—in this he also follows the lead of von List.

Gorsleben, who fought in the First World War on the western front and in a German unit attached to the Turkish army in Arabia, was very active in the political right after the war. He was originally a member of the Thule Society, but soon tired of the political infighting and turned his attention to more esoteric matters. On November 29, 1925 he founded the Edda Society in his home in Dinkelsbühl. The Grand Master of the Society was Werner von Bülow; Friedrich Schaefer was its treasurer. Schaefer's home was also the meeting place of a circle gathered around Karl Maria Wiligut in the early 1930s. Also members of the Edda Society were Otto Sigfrid Reuter and Mathilde von Kemnitz, who would marry General Ludendorff and become the spiritual leader of the society dedicated to him. Gorsleben also edited a newspaper called *Deutsche Freiheit* (German Freedom), which changed its name to *Arische Freiheit* (Aryan Freedom) in 1927.

According to Gorsleben's vision, the zenith of power of the Aryan race, originally manifested in an antediluvian Golden Age, is to be remanifested through a combination of eugenics and the systematic reawakening of occult powers and abilities. In this he was hardly original; but he saw the runes as the key to this reawakening. The runes were seen by Gorsleben much in the same way that Marby and others saw them—as tools for the reception and transmission of subtle occult forces in the universe. It is through them that the "people of the runes" and the ultimate powers in the universe may commune, thereby constantly bringing those who use the runes into a greater level of universal power.

Chiefly through his voluminous book, Gorsleben exercised a great influence on subsequent rune occultists. *Die Hoch-Zeit der Menschheit* was reprinted in Germany in the early 1980s, and it continues to make its influence felt.

Friedrich Bernhard Marby (Υ May 10, 1882, Aurich– ⋏ December 3, 1966, Stuttgart) could be considered one of the three great innovative figures in the history of German runic occultism. The others would be Guido von List and Rudolf John Gorsleben. He was certainly the first to publish extensively the practical applications of the runes in magical work. It was Marby who apparently first began to employ the runes as a psychosomatic system of gathering and channelling rune might throughout the personal sphere and among bodies in the cosmos. This system was called *Runengymnastik* (runic gymnastics) by him, but Siegfried Adolf Kummer called his system based on the same idea *Runenyoga* (runic yoga).

The details of Marby's life are fairly well known. (I am indebted to documents made available to me by Herr Rudolf Arnold Spieth.) Marby was originally a printer and editor by trade. He was apprenticed to a press in Hannover in 1896 and remained in Hannover until 1915. In 1906 he was married to a woman whom he later called "Else" in his writings. By his own accounts it was in 1907 that he first started working with the runes in esoteric ways. But it was not until 1911 that his researches had progressed to the point where he could actually talk about them. The dates are significant in that if Marby had begun his runic studies in 1907—one year prior to the appearance of Guido von List's landmark study *The Secret of the Runes*—then he could have claimed to have begun on the runic path independent of von List. However, even if he did begin his studies at that time, it cannot be denied that the Listian system had some influence on his development between 1907 and 1911.

Marby eventually made his way to Stuttgart, where he worked on the *Württemberger Zeitung*. In 1922 he published his first works concerning astrology and runic esotericism. That same year he gave up his regular profession to devote himself fully to his esoteric work and to publication in that field. In 1924 he began to publish the newspaper *Der eigene Weg* (Our Own Way), which dealt mostly with astrological questions. Marby founded a society called Orion, which gave him many opportunities to deliver lectures throughout the country.

It was in 1928 that Marby really started to delve deeply into the traditions of the North. Marby was of Swedish and Frisian extraction, and it was at this time that he undertook a trip to his ancestral homeland in Rimbo, Sweden. Two years later he also made a trip to Holte, Denmark. These trips supported his research into the practical applications of the power of the runes. After this period of traveling he returned to Germany in 1933 and began to concentrate more fully on rune work. He became very well known for his runic investigations, and this reputation made a sprinkling of enemies for him—many more than any of his astrological studies had made.

From 1931 to 1935 Marby published four double volumes of his runic researches in his *Marby-Runen-Bücherei* (Marby Runic Library). During this time he also founded the League of Runic Researchers, which largely worked by correspondence and which coordinated daily projections of rune might between all its members. According to figures published by Marby in 1932, there were 200 members of the League at that time.

Of course, by 1933 the National Socialists were in

power in Germany. In 1935 Marby returned to Stuttgart and continued his rune work. The National Socialists had tolerated his work up to a point, and indeed Marby had been a vocal supporter of Nazi ideology in the early years; but apparently when it became obvious that Marby would remain an independent voice in the field of occultism, he was arrested and tried in 1936. He spent the duration of the war in concentration camps. Two things were clear about Marby's arrest and detention: (1) if he were to talk about certain things and the involvement of certain people in his work, he would be secretly killed, and (2) if he did cooperate with the Nazis, he would leave the concentration camp alive. All his property was seized and his presses were destroyed. Ultimately he spent a total of 99 months in the camps Welzheim, Flossenberg, and Dachau. He was liberated from Dachau on April 29, 1945.

Marby did not receive any financial restitution for the losses caused by the Nazis' persecution, because it was found that he, too, had made anti-Jewish statements in print and had in the beginning supported the Nazis. It was not until 1952 that Marby was able to continue his work, publishing the periodical *Forschung und Erfahrung* until his death in 1966.

Marby and some of his followers spent much time and effort in trying to show that he was the original rune esotericist, and in charging others in the field with plagiarism. This seems rather strange in a way, since Marby and others claimed to be reviving ancient forms of folk wisdom, which seems a difficult thing to copyright. In the early phase of his career these charges were primarily directed against S. A. Kummer, who apparently had some early contact with Marby's practices, although Marby never claimed that Kummer was his student.

Kummer created a system of rune magic more harmonious with the system of runology taught by Guido von

List. He considered himself an Armanist, and more strictly used the 18-rune futhork of List in his work. Kummer (ᛉ 1899) is a rather mysterious figure, and little is known of his life. In 1927 he founded the Rune-School Runa near Dresden, where he taught his techniques of rune magic. It is known that he (along with Marby) was criticized by name in a report by Karl Wiligut to Reichsführer SS Heinrich Himmler, but what his fate was is unknown. There is at least one report that he is in exile in South America.

In the "high tide" of the runic renaissance there were dozens of writers and private occultists dealing with the runes. Every sort of magical school, it seemed, had to come to terms with them. It was during this time that the most influential eclectic magical lodge in Germany, the Fraternitas Saturni, began to incorporate runic occultism into its magical curriculum.

In the 1920s and early 1930s the runes had found a broad and powerful field of activity; but the bitter edge ground on the runic sword, and perhaps the lack of a wise leader to wield it magically, laid down the law, leading to woeful *wyrd*.

Chapter 4

The Swastika and the Runes

Much has been made of the supposed occult connections of the leading members of the National Socialist movement. By far the best account of this subject is Nicholas Goodrick-Clarke's *The Occult Roots of Nazism*. It is always a difficult task to unravel the threads of historical fact from fiction and propaganda when the subject is that of magical or esoteric orders. This difficulty is doubled when the world of power politics is thrown into the mix. What is clear is that the leaders of the Nazi Party were themselves as much shaped by the current of *völkisch* politics and Neo-Romantic mysticism, with its heavy admixture of Teutonic myth and magic, as they were shapers and re-shapers of that great mass movement in central Europe. They took what was essentially a diffuse mass mood and set of predilections that were just beginning to gel into a coherent cultural movement and channeled it into a specific, partisan institution: the National Socialist German Workers Party (NSDAP). In a way, if we think for a moment of "Germanticism" as a product, they schemed to get a corner on the market and, eventually, to monopolize it. This only became possible with the full force of the government at their command.

As soon as the Nazis came to power in 1933, esoteric lodges and organizations were banned and suppressed. The groups with a Germanic orientation were in some cases better treated in the beginning—that is, unless they had direct links to the NSDAP, such as the Thule Society, of which many of the early members of the Party were a part. The earliest book detailing the occult-Nazi connection was written by one of the Party's members, Rudolf von Sebottendorf, who wrote *Bevor Hitler kam* (Before Hitler Came). In this book, Sebottendorf made exaggerated claims regarding the level of the Party's involvement with his own esoteric ideas. The book was promptly banned and burned.

Other men and organizations were allowed to continue their work until the outbreak of the war in 1939. For example, Werner von Bülow continued to publish *Hagal*, the official organ of the Edda Society, until that year. However, it was far more typical for the bureaucracy to eventually catch up to the groups and put an end to their activities. This was the fate of F. B. Marby, which I have already detailed.

The study of the runes themselves was complex and multifaceted during the years of the Third Reich. There were essentially three levels to this study: (1) the purely academic-scientific, (2) the lay-scientific, and (3) the esoteric. Those involved in academic circles received more attention than ever before but were left largely unencumbered by politics to pursue their scientific ends. This fact shows that on one level the Nazis realized these studies had some validity. However, they also installed men who had formerly been lay investigators (self-appointed experts without academic credentials) in academic posts. The details of this phase of the work of the *Ahnenerbe* of the SS and of the *Institut für Runenforschung* (Institute for Runic Research) are to be found in Ulrich Hunger's dissertation

Runenkunde im Dritten Reich. But it is the third, or esoteric, level of study that interests us most here. This information was very limited and highly sensitive, even within the confines of Party politics, and therefore quite secret.

Essentially, the truly magical or esoteric applications of the runes and rune magic as such seems to have been the main interest of Reichsführer SS Heinrich Himmler. In this pursuit his chief adviser was the mysterious Karl Maria Weisthor—sometimes called "Himmler's Rasputin." Among other things, Weisthor was the designer of the runic rings worn by the Death's Head SS officers and the main adviser for the acquisition and planning of the Wewelsburg citadel—secret headquarters of the SS and officially designated as its officers' college.

But who was this Weisthor, and where did he come from? This information was obscure at the time, and intentionally so, for he was actually none other than Karl Maria Wiligut (ᛟ December 10, 1866, Vienna– ᛉ January 3, 1946), also known as Jarl Widar and Lobesam. He had been active in esoteric runic circles in Germany and Austria beginning around the time of his retirement from the Austrian army in 1919. Actually Wiligut's career in the world of runic mysticism had started much earlier with the publication of his book entitled *Seyfrids Runen*, which seems to have been influenced by the early ideas of Guido von List. Wiligut claimed to be the descendant/reincarnation of the king of the ancient Asa-Uana-Sippe (clan), to have been initiated into the secrets of his family traditions in 1890, and to have written the Nine Commandments of Gode in 1908. These Nine Commandments are

1. Gode is Al-unity!
2. Gode is "spirit and matter," the dyad. He brings duality, and is, nevertheless, unity and purity.

3. Gode is a triad: spirit, energy, and matter. Gode-spirit, Gode-Ur, Gode-being, or Sun-light and Waker, the dyad.

4. Eternal is Gode—as time, space, energy, and matter in his circulating current.

5. Gode is cause and effect. Therefore, out of Gode flows right, might, duty, and happiness.

6. Gode is eternally generating. The matter, energy, and light of Gode are that which carry this along.

7. Gode—beyond the concepts of good and evil—is that which carries the seven epochs of human history.

8. Rulership in the circulation of the current carries along the Highness—the secret tribunal.

9. Gode is beginning without end—the Al. He is completion in nothingness and, nevertheless, Al in the three times three realization of all things. He closes the circle at N-Yule, at nothingness, out of the conscious into the unconscious, so that this may again become conscious.

Here the peculiar spellings of *Gode* for "God" and *Al* for "All" reflect the peculiarities of Wiligut's own usages. Wiligut claimed that these were the commandments that had been orally transmitted along family lines within the Asa-Uana-Sippe for 1200 years.

From his retirement home in Salzburg, Wiligut developed a following of students of his traditions in the early 1920s. His teachings remained private and secret, but they have been documented by several students. However, Wiligut's unorthodox beliefs, coupled with marital problems and some bad business deals, seem to have resulted in his family having him declared mentally incompetent, and from 1924 to 1927 he was involuntarily confined to a mental institution. After his release Wiligut found his way to Germany and eventually became the focus of a runic study circle near Munich. Apparently Wiligut now used the name

Karl Maria Weisthor, and wrote under the name Jarl Widar, in an attempt to conceal his embarrassing past. When the Nazis came to power, one of Wiligut's students, Richard Anders, introduced him to Heinrich Himmler and Wiligut subsequently was inducted into the SS in September of 1933. From that time to August of 1939 "Weisthor" was Himmler's chief adviser on esoteric and magical matters. Unfortunately for Weisthor, his past was eventually discovered by those below Himmler. Although Himmler certainly knew the facts of the matter and had helped cover them up, the political pressure was sufficient that Wiligut was forced to resign his post in the SS. The elderly Wiligut was cared for in his retirement by the SS, but he succumbed to the physical strains imposed by conditions right after the end of the war.

Wiligut may have been instrumental in the suppression of other runic magicians in Germany (such as Kummer and Marby) and in the protection of the Edda Society (of which he was a member). The bulk of Wiligut's written record is largely philosophical and cosmological/meta-historical. In this his work is closely akin to that of Guido von List, but as it does not directly relate to the subject of practical rune magic, we must leave it for now.

For the most part the runes were used in a less magical way by the NSDAP—that is, they were used as emotionally loaded symbols and signs that appealed to the mass of the Germanophilic population and repelled and terrorized the Germanophobic. Of course, the swastika itself belongs to this group of symbols. Guido von List had already identified the 18th rune, GIBOR ⌁ , as a "concealed swastika" long before it was adopted, at the suggestion of Adolf Hitler himself, as the official insignia of the NSDAP in 1920. Although the Nazis never developed an actual National Socialist runology, certain features are evident. The SIG-rune was the rune of victory (G. *Sieg*), the TYR-rune was the rune of the struggle (G. *Kampf*), the OTHIL-rune was the symbol of "blood and soil," and the HAGAL-rune was that of salvation (or racial purity).

The National Socialist episode in the history of the runic revival is a clear example of the inherent power of the runes and how that power, which is essentially rooted in the soul of the folk, will eventually resist any attempts to force it to conform to any partisan cause other than that for which the runes stand: the well-being of the folk and the seeking of wisdom. It is clear from the results that the Nazi Party violated these principles on both counts.

Figure 4.1 Design of the Death's Head Ring by Wiligut

Chapter 5

From the Ashes:
A New Runic Revival

I n the years immediately after the Second World War, and to some extent continuing to the present day, the runes were so closely associated with the Nazis that the use and discussion of them in academic as well as esoteric circles was hampered by adverse public opinion. Those of the old rune magicians who had survived the war in Germany slowly began to make their way back to their work, and new voices were also heard.

The best known of these new voices is Karl Spiesberger. He published his groundbreaking rune-magic synthesis in 1955, *Runenmagie* (Rune Magic). Spiesberger was an initiate of the Fraternitas Saturni (Fra∴Eratus), and his work is surely based on that order's understanding of the runes. Spiesberger, like most authors on esoteric or magical subjects, presented a mixture of the old with some original innovations of his own. To some extent the innovations may have been drawn from the teachings of the Fraternitas Saturni. What Spiesberger essentially tried to do was remove the racist aspects of the Armanic and Marbyan rune work and place the whole system in a pansophical, or eclectic, context. To a List, Marby, or Kummer the runes represented THE KEY to esoteric understanding; to Spiesberger they are just one more tool to be used by the individual magician. Spiesberger's works are always cast in the 18-rune futhork as originally envisioned by Guido von List and magically developed by S. A. Kummer.

Another exponent of the new runic revival was Roland Dionys Jossé, who published a work, also in 1955, called *Die Tala der Raunen*. In this work he made use of the 16-rune futhark, which was a major historical departure for the practice of runic esotericism in Germany. Jossé rightly assumed that the 17th and 18th runes of the "Hávamál" (taken up by List as gospel) were actually additional runes lying outside the numerological system. Jossé presents a complex but highly workable form of practical runic numerology and a system of astrology based on the formula of 16.

The numerology can be simply explained as a system of first transliterating a person's name into the 16 runes of the Younger Futhark, then reducing it to a key number by "units" of 16, adding the remainder until a number below 16 (or 18) is reached. For example, the name Robert Zoller would be treated in the following manner:

$$=87=16\times5+7=12$$

That is, there are five units of 16 in the sum of the numerical values of the name (16 x 5), with seven left over. These are added to the number of units to arrive at the key number of the name, which is 12. Therefore the key-rune for this individual, according to this system, would be the TYR-rune.

The greatest of the rune sages to survive the upheavals of the Nazi period was F. B. Marby, of course. He continued to publish works relevant to his *Marby-Runen-Gymnastik*. In 1957 he came out with what is perhaps his greatest work, *Die drei Schwäne* (The Three Swans), which had been completed before his arrest by the Nazis in 1936. This book is a kind of mystical autobiography, and as published in 1957, it contains copious notes and commentaries by the author that make it invaluable in understanding the Marbyan system.

The Runes in Germany Today

No other land is more esoterically bound up with the runes than Germany is. Since the dawn of the occult revival in Germany the runes have been playing their part in that revival. Therefore, when we look at the ways in which the runes are used in magical circles in Germany today, we see a deep-level network of interconnections that is much richer, but also more diffuse, than that which we might find in England or the United States. There is at least one order active in Germany that is based on what are essentially runic ideas: the Armanen Orden. The magical order Fraternitas Saturni, which maintains an eclectic magical curriculum, probably also continues to have as a part of that curriculum instruction in the art of rune magic. But beyond this there is a variety of individual magicians teaching and learning runic techniques that are used as just one part of an eclectic magical repertoire.

The Armanen Orden was for all intents and purposes a moribund institution before it was revived by Adolf Schleipfer in 1968. He received the charter of the order from the then-aged president of the Guido von List Society and proceeded to rebuild it based on what seems to be a syncretization of the ideas of not only List but also the other rune mystics and magicians of the German past (Marby, Kummer, Gorsleben, etc.), as well as the traditions of the Order of the New Templars and the Fraternitas Saturni. The rune magic of the Armanen continues to be taught mostly within the confines of the Armanen Orden itself.

Another almost exclusively rune-based system is that of Marby-Rune-Gymnastics. This magical system continues to be promoted through the works of F. B. Marby, as published by the Spieth Verlag. Another school essentially based on the runic system is gathered around the works of Werner Kosbab.

By far, the majority of contemporary German rune magicians are exposed to the tradition through published literature and by means of workshops, such as the ones held at Askona. There has been no real runic explosion in Germany as there has been in the English-speaking world, because the "explosion" already took place in the 1920s and early 1930s. But since the rise from the ashes of the past there has been a steady production of rune-based works. The new interest in runic esoterica in Germany comes in the form of that imported from English-speaking circles. Most of the current runic authors' works are finding their way into German translations.

The bibliography at the end of this book will show the history of publication of major rune books in Germany. But it is also important to note that rune teachers, such as Karl Spiesberger, also teach runic techniques in workshop and seminar settings. It is mostly through a combination of the widely available books on rune magic and the seminars offered to the public that the German-speaking world of today is exposed to the teachings of the runes.

In the past few years a new era has dawned, perhaps through a working of *wyrd*, in that the German occult circles have been introduced to the magical traditions of the Elder Futhark through the translations of my own works and the original works of Frater V∴,D∴..

As a footnote to the contemporary scene, it might be noted that the Rune-Gild in the USA and elsewhere promotes the knowledge of, and individual experimentation in, the Armanic and Marbyan forms of rune magic. The present study is just one facet of that work. However, the magical-initiatory system of the Rune-Gild continues to be primarily based in the purely traditional forms of historically authentic runelore.

One teacher, Karl Hans Welz of the Knights of Runes, teaches a purely Armanic tradition of rune magic in America. He was a student of Karl Spiesberger, and his system is completely lacking in any racist overtones.

Chapter 6

The Traditional Runic Systems

W hen looking at the runic traditions from an occult point of view, we see that there are actually four systems to take into account:

1) The Elder Futhark (24 runes)
2) The Anglo-Frisian Futhorc (29–33 runes)
3) The Younger Futhark (16 runes)
4) The Armanic Futhork (18 runes)

The first three of these have deep historical roots, while the fourth system is the result of the occult vision of Guido von List. However, all four systems can be seen for what they are: various facets of the underlying runic reality, of which these systems are the most external phenomena. The fact that there is a degree of fluctuation in the traditions is perhaps to be expected of the Teutonic magical systems, which so highly value the state of flux and resulting growth. In this book various techniques are based on one or the other of these systems. Therefore the "runester" should be familiar with the fundamentals of all of them and with how they all fit together to form the whole of the occult runic tradition.

Table 6.1 The 24-Rune System

No.	Sound	Shape	Name
1	f	ᚠ	*fehu*
2	u	ᚢ	*uruz*
3	th	ᚦ	*thurisaz*
4	a	ᚨ	*ansuz*
5	r	ᚱ	*raidho*
6	k	ᚲ	*kenaz*
7	g	ᚷ	*gebo*
8	w	ᚹ	*wunjo*
9	h	ᚺ	*hagalaz*
10	n	ᚾ	*nauthiz*
11	i	ᛁ	*isa*
12	j/y	ᛃ	*jera*
13	i	ᛇ	*ihwaz*
14	p	ᛈ	*perthro*
15	-z/-R	ᛉ	*elhaz*
16	s	ᛊ	*sowilo*
17	t	ᛏ	*tiwaz*
18	b	ᛒ	*berkano*
19	e	ᛖ	*ehwaz*
20	m	ᛗ	*mannaz*
21	l	ᛚ	*laguz*
22	ng	ᛜ	*ingwaz*
23	d	ᛞ	*dagaz*
24	o	ᛟ	*othila*

Table 6.1   The 24-Rune System (cont.)

No.	Exoteric Meaning	Esoteric Meaning
1	Livestock→Money	Dynamic power
2	Aurochs (wild bison)	Vital formative essence
3	Thurs (giant)	Breaker of resistance
4	A God (Woden)	Sovereign ancestral force
5	Wagon/Chariot	Vehicle on path to cosmic power
6	Torch	Controlled energy
7	Gift (sacrifice)	Exchanged force
8	Joy/pleasure	Harmony of like forces
9	Hail(-stone)	Seed form and primal union
10	Need (distress)	Need-Fire (friction/liberation)
11	Ice	Contraction (matter/anti-matter)
12	Year (harvest)	Orbit (life cycle)
13	Yew tree	Axis (tree of life/death)
14	Lot-cup	Evolutionary force
15	Elk	Protective and tutelary beings
16	Sun	Sun-wheel (crystallized light)
17	The God Tyr	Sovereign order
18	Birch(-goddess)	Birch numen (container/releaser)
19	Horse	Twin equine gods (trust)
20	Man(-kind)	Human order of divine origin
21	Water	Life force and organic growth
22	Ing, the Earth God	Gestation/container
23	Day	Dawn/twilight (paradox)
24	Ancestral property	Self-contained hereditary power

The Elder Futhark

Actually no specific technique outlined in this book makes direct use of the Elder Futhark; however, from a historical and traditional point of view, the Elder Futhark of 24 runes is the oldest and most original of all the systems. It is the foundation and root from which the others developed and grew. The primacy of this system is clear for all to see who take the trouble to look up the history of runology in any standard (non-occult) reference work. Those who want deeper instruction in this system are directed to my own works cited in the bibliography of this book, and to the Rune-Gild, which makes exclusive use of this system in its rune work. Donald Tyson also employs a form of this tradition in his books, but other than these, all the other occult works that purport to make use of the 24-rune system are fundamentally flawed and are of little traditional magical value.

The system of 24 runes, as seen in Table 6.1, was used in ancient times from the dim beginnings of the runic tradition to about 800 C.E. in both Scandinavia and Germany. At that time there was a smooth and regular transition to the 16-rune system of the Younger Futhark in Scandinavia. In this table, as in those for all the other systems, the numerical value, name, phonetic value, shape, the exoteric meaning (the literal translation of the name), and the esoteric meaning (the underlying significance of that name in the runic context) are given.

The Anglo-Frisian Futhorc

In historical terms the Anglo-Frisian Futhorc was in use from as early as 400 C.E. well into the Middle Ages, when it was preserved in manuscripts, and perhaps beyond. Its original homeland was in present-day Holland and northern Germany, the ancient region inhabited by the Frisians, Angles, and Saxons. From there it was brought to England in the middle of the fifth century.

The systemic principle of the Anglo-Frisian Futhorc is *expansion*. It is simply an extension of the Elder Futhark, with some sound-value modifications. As the exoteric and esoteric vocabulary of the Anglo-Frisians expanded, so too did they expand their runic system. They simply added those signs they needed on to the end of the rune-row. This apparently came in two phases, first expanding to 29 runes (exemplified in the Anglo-Saxon Rune Poem) and eventually to a total of 33 runes. This latter tradition was especially prevalent in the manuscript runes.

From an esoteric standpoint it is clear that those who were responsible for expanding the Anglo-Frisian Futhorc were deeply initiated into the Teutonic mysteries. This is true even of those who expanded the row to its ultimate length of 33 runestaves. It is an intriguing fact that the final three runes in this row—the cup, the stone, and the spear—refer directly to the Graal-Mythos. But this reference would appear to be a particularly Teutonic understanding, with double meanings for each of these symbols. The cup is both the sacred drinking vessel from which Woden's mead of inspiration is drunk and the cup used at the Last Supper, which was taken to Britain by Joseph of Arimathaea: the Christian Grail. The stone is the stone altar of sacrifice, but also the *stone* Graal, as described exclusively in the medieval German tradition of Wolfram von Eschenbach. In this tradition the Graal is said to have been a stone that fell from Lucifer's crown during the war in heaven between Lucifer and the Trinity. The stone was then brought to earth by a band of "doubting angels," who took neither side in this war. On earth it is guarded and cared for by a secret order of chivalry. The spear is first and foremost the Germanic symbol of sovereign and divine authority, and also the main

Table 6.2 The Anglo-Frisian Futhorc

No.	Sound	Shape	Name	Exoteric Meaning
1	f	ᚠ	*feoh*	cattle, wealth
2	u	ᚢ	*ur*	wild ox
3	th/dh	ᚦ	*thorn*	thorn
4	o	ᚩ	*os*	a god (or mouth)
5	r	ᚱ	*rad*	(a) ride
6	c/ch	ᚳ	*cen*	torch
7	g [j/zh]	ᚷ	*gyfu*	gift
8	w	ᚹ	*wynn*	joy
9	h	ᚻ	*hægl*	hail
10	n	ᚾ	*nyd*	need, distress
11	i	ᛁ	*is*	ice
12	y	ᛄ	*ger*	year
13	eo	ᛇ	*eoh*	yew
14	p	ᛈ	*peordh*	dice-box
15	x	ᛉ	*eolhx*	elks/sedge-reed
16	s	ᛋ	*sigel*	sun

Table 6.2 The Anglo-Frisian Futhorc (cont.)

17	t	↑	*tir*	Tiw/sign or glory
18	b	ᛒ	*beorc*	birch/poplar
19	e	ᛖ	*eh*	horse
20	m	ᛗ	*monn*	man (human being)
21	l	ᛚ	*lagu*	sea
22	ng	ᛝ	*ing*	the god Ing
23	d	ᛞ	*dæg*	day
24	e [ay]	ᛟ	*ethel*	ancestral property
25	a	ᚪ	*ac*	oak
26	æ	ᚫ	*æsc*	ash
27	y	ᚣ	*yr*	gold decoration/bow
28	ea	ᛠ	*ear*	earth-grave
29	eo/io	ᛡ	*ior*	serpent
30	q	ᛢ	*(c)weordh*	fire-twirl
31	k	ᛣ	*calc*	chalk/cup
32	st	ᛥ	*stan*	stone
33	g	ᚸ	*gar*	spear

Table 6.2   The Anglo-Frisian Futhorc (cont.)

No.	Esoteric Meaning
1	Dynamic power
2	Vital formative essence
3	Breaker of resistance
4	Sovereign ancestral force
5	Vehicle on path to cosmic power
6	Controlled energy
7	Exchanged force
8	Harmony of like forces
9	Seed form and primal union
10	Need-Fire (friction/liberation)
11	Contraction (matter/anti-matter)
12	Orbit (life cycle)
13	Axis (tree of life/death)
14	Evolutionary force
15	Protective and tutelary beings
16	Sun-wheel (crystallized light)
17	Sovereign order
18	Birch numen (container/releaser)
19	Twin equine gods (trust)
20	Human order of divine origin
21	Life force and organic growth
22	Gestation/container
23	Dawn/twilight (paradox)
24	Self-contained hereditary power
25	Sacred oak
26	Primal human material (the ash/elm trees)
27	Primal entity (Ymir)
28	Cosmic containment (the Midgard-Serpent)
29	Ritual interment (reabsorption by nature)
30	Ritual altar fire
31	Ritual container (Graal-Cup)
32	Ritual stone altar (Graal-Stone)
33	Ritual spear (spear of Woden/Parzival)

weapon of Woden. In the Christian mythos it is the spear that the Roman soldier Longinus used to stab Jesus as he hung on the cross. This is also supposed to be a part of the Graal reliquary.

In occult circles, Friedrich Bernhard Marby made use of the 33-rune Anglo-Frisian Futhorc, which he taught was the primeval runic system inherited from the Atlantean Mother-Land (Thule), which goes back to an age some 12,000 years distant in the past. In his published writings Marby never undertook a systematic delineation of his whole runic system. Instead, his works on runic gymnastics abound with the practice of individual runic exercises for the key I-rune (see chapter 7) and for the vowel sounds that he identifies as "Hall-Runes" (resonant runes). More recently, a somewhat more traditional view of the Anglo-Frisian system has been outlined by Marijane Osborn and Stella Longland in their book *Rune Games*.

The Younger Futhark

The 16-rune system of the Younger Futhark was historically in use throughout the Viking Age (between about 800 and 1150 C.E. Knowledge of this system was preserved in secret throughout the Christianized Medieval Age, even though cultural forces attempted to destroy the runic tradition in its true form. The Younger Futhark is an unusual and conscious reformation of the Elder Futhark system. It is highly unusual that at a time when the Scandinavian dialects were becoming linguistically more complex and developing more sounds, the writing system used to represent this language was simplified by reducing the number of signs available to represent those sounds. This is almost unheard of in the history of alphabets. What made this possible was the fact that the runes were not being reformed by or for those who were interested in maintaining a utilitarian script.

Table 6.3 The Younger Futhark

No.	Sound	Shape	Name
1	f	ᚠ	*fé*
2	u/o/v	ᚢ	*úr*
3	th/dh	ᚦ	*thurs*
4	a	ᚭ	*áss*
5	r	ᚱ	*reidh*
6	k/g/ng	ᚴ	*kaun*
7	h	ᚼ	*hagall*
8	n	ᚾ	*naudh*
9	i/e	ᛁ	*íss*
10	a	ᛅ	*ár*
11	s	ᛋ	*sól*
12	t/d/nd	ᛏ	*Týr*
13	b/p/mb	ᛒ	*bjarkan*
14	m	ᛘ	*madhr*
15	l	ᛚ	*lögr*
16	-R	ᛦ	*ýr*

Table 6.3 The Younger Futhark (cont.)

No.	Exoteric Meaning	Esoteric Meaning
1	cattle, money, gold	dynamic power
2	drizzling rain/aurochs	fertilizing essence
3	thurs (giant)	breaker of resistance
4	*the* god (=Ódhinn)	word-power, sovereign force
5	a ride, thunderclap	spiritual path or journey
6	a sore	internal fire or protection
7	hail	ice seed form
8	need, bondage, fetters	need-fire, slavery/freedom
9	ice	contraction prima materia
10	(good) year, harvest	blooming into manifestation
11	sun	sun wheel/crystallized light
12	the god Týr	sovereign heavenly order
13	birch (-goddess)	gestation/birth
14	man, human	ancestral divine order
15	sea, waterfall	life energy/organic growth
16	yew, bow of yew wood	telluric power

It was reformed by those more akin to priests (the runemasters) than to scribes or grammarians. The signs were reduced in number according to an orderly method in which the symbolic values of the runes that were eliminated were absorbed by the remaining ones. Thus a streamlined system was created.

The Younger Futhark has been the least-used by the modern occult revival. The numerological work of Roland Dionys Jossé is, however, based on the 16 runes of the Younger Futhark. It is also important to realize that the 18-rune system of Guido von List and the Armanists is really an extension of the Younger Futhark.

The Armanic Futhork

The 18 runes of the Armanic Futhork have a purely esoteric heritage. This system originated with the occult vision of Guido von List, who based the system on the 18 runic stanzas in the Eddic poem "Hávamál"—"Sayings of the High One." List claimed to have esoteric knowledge that the 18-rune futhork was indeed the primeval system from which all others were derived. Although no historian or philologist would agree, the Armanic system did become the main one used by German rune magicians and esoteric philosophers. It was the basis for S. A. Kummer's practical work (which he characterized as Armanic), it was accepted by Gorsleben and used as the basis for his runic investigations, and it was generally accepted as traditional among most German rune occultists. Because of this wide acceptance and the decades of magical practice supporting it, the system has acquired a great storehouse of occult power. The greatest postwar popularizer of rune magic, Karl Spiesberger, also used the 18-rune system in a way most similar to that employed by Kummer. The only significant non-Armanic rune magician, and the only man to steer his own way through the seas of German runic esotericism, was F. B. Marby, who made use of the Anglo-Frisian system mentioned above.

In Table 6.4 the Armanic Futhork is presented, but because it is fundamentally different in nature from the other historical rows, it must be treated in a somewhat different way. The names of the runes are really thought of as kernel- or seed-words from which the so-called Aryo-Germanic language developed and according to which esoteric meanings of modern words may be derived. There is no room in this study to delve into this complex body of occult lore, which rivals the complexity of the Hebrew Kabbalah.

Table 6.4   The Armanic Futhork

No.	Shape	Name	Meaning
1	ᚠ	FA	Primal fire, change, re-shaping, banishing of distress, sending generative principle, primal spirit
2	ᚢ	UR	Eternity, consistency, physician's rune, luck, telluric magnetism, primal soul
3	ᚦ	THORN	Action, will to action, evolutionary power, goal-setting, rune of Od-magnetic transference
4	ᚨ	OS	Breath, spiritual well-being, word, radiating od-magnetic power
	ᛜ	OTHIL	Arising, the power of the word, the receptive power
5	ᚱ	RIT	Primal law, rightness, advice, rescue, rhythm
6	ᚲ	KA	Generation, power, art, ability, propagation
7	ᚼ	HAGAL	All-enclosure, spiritual leadership, protectiveness, harmony, cosmic order, the midpoint of order
8	ᚾ	NOT	The unavoidable, karma, compulsion of fate
9	ᛁ	IS	Ego, will, activity, personal power, banishing, consciousness of spiritual power, control of self and others
10	ᛉ	AR	Sun, wisdom, beauty, virtue, fame, well-being, protection from specters, leadership
11	ᛋ	SIG	Solar power, victory, success, knowledge, realization, power to actualize
12	ᛏ	TYR	Power, success, wisdom, generation, awakening, rebirth in the spirit, spiraling development

Table 6.4 The Armanic Futhork (cont.)

13	ᛒ	BAR	Becoming, birth, the third birth in the spirit, concealment, song
14	ᛚ	LAF	Primal law, life, experience of life, love, primal water, water and ocean rune
15	ᛉ	MAN	Man-rune, increase, fullness, health, magic, spirit, god-man, the masculine principle in the cosmos, day-consciousness
16	ᛦ	YR	Woman-rune, instinct, greed, passion, matter, delusion, confusion, death, destruction, the negative feminine principle in the cosmos, night-consciousness
17	ᛇ	EH	Marriage, lasting love, law, justice, hope, duration, rune of trust and of the dual (twin) souls
18	ᚷ	GIBOR	God-rune, god-all, cosmic consciousness, wedding together of powers, the generative and receptive, sacred marriage, giver and the gift, fulfillment

In essence there are only these four true runic systems. Other pseudo-systems have been been invented out of whole cloth, or aspects of the systems have been significantly distorted by recent writers, especially in the Anglo-American market. I do not feel it is necessary to address any of these systems or their aberrations. What is needed, however, is a systemic synthesis of the four legitimate rune-magic traditions. Once such a synthetic understanding is gained, it will be easier for the runester to make use of the magical practices and lore particular to each of the systems, while maintaining a solid base of traditionally anchored knowledge. There can be no doubt, from any point of view, that the 24-rune Elder Futhark is the oldest and most original of all the traditions. It is the primary thesis, which actually represents the original Teutonic synthesis of universal knowledge. It is from a knowledge-base in this system that a synthetic understanding of all the other systems is most easily achieved.

Although there are esoteric and cosmological keys to unlocking the internal relationships of these four systems, it is more the purpose of this book to look to the practical use of *individual* runes and certain runic combinations as taught by the German rune magicians of the early part of this century. Therefore I keep cosmological speculations to a minimum.

Those who have been schooled, or who have schooled themselves, in the tradition of the Elder Futhark will note that qualities of the Armanic system relate to the 24-rune system in approximately the ways outlined in Table 6.5.

Keep in mind that these are not strict equivalents but only rough correspondences. The elder tradition can teach the runester much more about the Armanic system than the Armanic system can be used to understand the older tradition.

As they are both products of the human spirit, much as

Table 6.5
The Relationship of the Armanic Tradition to that of the Elder Futhark

No. Rune	Armanic Rune	Approximate symbolic equivalent in the Elder Futhark
1	FA	*fehu*
2	UR	*uruz*
3	THORN	*thurisaz*
4	OS/OTHIL	*ansuz, othila*
5	RIT	*raidho*
6	KA	*kenaz*
7	HAGAL	*hagalaz, dagaz, wunjo*
8	NOT	*nauthiz*
9	IS	*isa*
10	AR	*jera*
11	SIG	*sowilo*
12	TYR	*tiwaz*
13	BAR	*berkano, perthro, ingwaz*
14	LAF	*laguz/laukaz*
15	MAN	*mannaz, elhaz* (positive aspects)
16	YR	*ihwaz, elhaz* (negative aspects)
17	EH	*ehwaz*
18	GIBOR	*gebo*

---

language is, each of these two systems can be translated into one another. But as with all translations, there is a good deal of art in the process, and no perfect translation is really possible. Although they may be dialects of the same basic language, each have high degrees of internal integrity that keep them independent of one another. The runester dedicated to the investigation of the authentic ancient runic traditions should approach the material in this book cautiously, taking useful practical techniques and leaving the cosmology and speculation on the system to others. The advantage of the Armanic system to magicians within the Western tradition of magic, who are not dedicated to a Teutonic path of initiation, is that the Armanic system is more a phenomenon of the general occult revival spanning the nineteenth and twentieth centuries than is the tradition of the Elder Futhark, which is far more a unique creature of the Teutonic world. I must add that although the Armanic tradition is a modern phenomenon, it remains a thoroughly Teutonic one.

Part II

Secret Practices

Chapter 7

Rune Yoga

In my book *Futhark: A Handbook of Rune Magic*, I introduced the art of *stadhagaldr*, which is based on the Elder Futhark. This technique was originally pioneered by the German rune magicians, especially by F. B. Marby, but it probably has its roots in the magical postures and gestures used by the ancient Indo-Europeans. In Scandinavia it is still a folk custom to teach the alphabet to children by having them strike poses imitative of the shapes of the letters while making the sound each represents. In this way they quickly and thoroughly internalize the shapes and sounds. This may indeed be one of those customs handed down from runic times that is now again understood for the magical technique it always was.

As far as this rediscovery is concerned, it seems that Marby was the first to see the practical magical applications of this technique, which he called Runengymnastik. Unfortunately, in his long career he did not fully articulate his system throughout the runic spectrum, so his work often seems uneven and incomplete. S. A. Kummer more or less took Marby's technique and published a full system based on its use in the early 1930s, and thus he has become perhaps better known for the system than Marby himself.

Kummer called the technique Runenyoga. This kind of magic was further systematized in the works of Karl Spiesberger.

In this chapter I will guide the reader through the theory and practice of the art of rune yoga as taught by Marby, Kummer, and Spiesberger. If the chapter is *worked* through, the reader will gain a basic understanding of the technique, which can then be either applied to further rune work of a more traditional kind or employed to deepen other magical disciplines.

A Theory of Rune Yoga

It is very important to gain some understanding of the theoretical base for rune yoga, especially as taught by F. B. Marby, because it has to do with much of the theory of how several of the other magical techniques work. In these ideas we get a theory for the full, practical magical use of the mysterious and often obscure streams and fields of power present in the earth and in the atmosphere, streaming to us from the vast reaches of space.

According to Marby there are five cosmic zones to be reckoned with: (1) inner-earth space, (2) material earth space, (3) wave space, (4) cosmic space, and (5) super cosmic space (see Figure 7.1). The inner space of earth (Marby considered the possibility of the "Hollow Earth Theory") is a vast but contained zone of tranquil space that radiates energy. This is compared to the outermost zone of cosmic space, which is also tranquil and radiant. Cosmic space, zone four, is charged with radiations from the zone of cosmic space and is influenced by the physical bodies (stars, planets, etc.) that occupy it. Material earth space is the physical matter of the planet, which is heavily loaded with ancient forms of energy coursing though it in various patterns. Wave space is that zone just above the surface of the

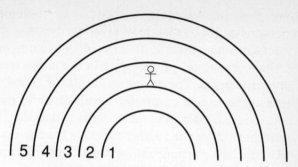

1. Inner Earth Space
2. Material Earth Space
3. Wave Space
4. Cosmic Space
5. Super Cosmic Space

Figure 7.1 The Five Zones of the Cosmos

earth that our bodies inhabit. This is the region where energy patterns received from above and below are most freely exchanged.

The rune magician makes him/herself capable of receiving and sending patterns of energy to and from all five of these zones. (Using the perhaps now quaint-sounding "high-tech" language of the early part of this century, the rune magician becomes an *antenna* for the reception and broadcast of runic radio waves.) By using the proper runic postures combined with the intonation of the right runic sound, the magician can draw in certain forces or combinations of forces and then reshape and redirect them. This, of course, takes great discipline and much work.

Although these ideas contain much that is traditional and quite ancient, they may be troublesome to those who see them as pseudoscientific. A word of encouragement to such persons might be that these ideas can be used simply to project subjective models onto the objective universe in order to effect magical phenomena in the subjective and objective universes. The usage of outdated terms is no worse than the use of computer terminology in magical contexts today. In fact, the speed with which the "high-tech" terminology of the 1920s and 1930s has become out-moded might be a warning as to what is likely to happen to the same kind of terminology of the 1980s.

The interplay of forces within these various energy zones constitutes the phenomena of the universe. By becoming aware of them, engaging them, and guiding them consciously, the rune magician actively participates in the evolution and restructuring of the cosmos.

The runes are the keys to the reception, absorption, and projection of these forces. Their first effect is on the transformation and healing of the individual. If a group—especially for the early German magicians, an ethnically/organically authentic *national* group—engages the runes as a body, that whole body will be gradually purified and strengthened. Marby himself hardly went beyond these motives in his published works. But beyond this, these forces can be used to any magical effect the runester wills.

In order for the runes to be effectively used, several factors must be taken into account: (1) shape (posture), (2) environmental space, (3) location (with relation to the surface of the globe), (4) direction or orientation, (5) stream of breath, (6) vocalic sound (vibration), (7) consonantal sound (vibration), (8) will (patterns of conscious thought), and perhaps also (9) motion (when shapes or postures are made dynamic). In this chapter we will concentrate on the practice of factor one and the basics of factors five and six. Chapter 10 will be concerned with the ninth factor, chapter 8 will take up factors five through seven in more detail, and chapter 12 will deal with factors of space, orientation, and location.

These nine basic factors, or "Nine Mothers" as Marby called them, are the keys to using the runes, which are the very *qualities* or *essences* of the powers themselves. The individual runic shapes and sounds are then the keys to the engagement and use of the individual qualities of power.

The Exercise of Rune Yoga

The First Runic Exercise

Before beginning any specialized rune work, the rune-ster must become familiar with the basic techniques. This is best done by means of the fundamental I-rune exercise. This exercise can be performed anywhere and at any time, and in the beginning it should be done as often as possible. The purpose of the exercise, besides the training aspect, is the general strengthening of the body and I-consciousness—a liberation from the dross elements and other limitations on the soul, resulting in an all-around rejuvenation. It can be performed in a standing position (which is most normal), while walking, or even sitting. If standing, you should keep your eyes focused straight ahead, chin down, chest out, with your feet forming a right angle to one another and the heels touching. If walking, keep your feet straight, your elbows slightly bent, and your palms facing forward in a slightly cupped position. The sitting form of the exercise is one where you sit straight in a chair, knees together, with your palms on your knees, and the arms held to the body. The only thought that should pervade your consciousness is "I-am-here." Practice often and in any location.

Marby's Eight-Step Introduction

The following eight-step introduction to the technique of runic gymnastics was first outlined by F. B. Marby in the first volume of his *Marby-Runen-Bücherei* (p. 72). As the intonation of the proper runic tones is also essential to the engagement of the runic forces, the basics of rune song will also be discussed here and elsewhere in this chapter. The full outline of the practice of runic mantras is found in the next chapter.

Remember that the I-rune exercise can be performed in a standing, walking, or sitting mode. Experiment to find the mode most effective for you.

1. Inhale for a time span of approximately five seconds. According to Marby this should be equivalent to the time it takes to walk about seven steps at a normal walking speed. Then exhale for an equal number of seconds. The main thing at this stage is to maintain a rhythm of breath that is comfortable for you. Slowly expand your abilities as you begin to be able to inhale for longer periods of time. Maintain a regular rhythm of breath. Practice as often as you can and in as many different places as you can.

2. Softly sing the *I* (pronounced in English "ee," as in "fee") sound. You should sing this in a tone and pitch most comfortable and natural to you. Maintain some tension in your lips so that your mouth is not too lax or broad. Practice daily in conjunction with the I-posture.

3. Once this comfortable and neutral tone has been mastered, practice raising the pitch of the note as high as you can. Do not pause in the raising of the pitch. Again, as with all exercises in rune song, the best measure of whether something is being done right is if it feels right and powerful to you.

4. Next try expanding the length of the initial *I*-sound to approximately ten seconds, or for about twelve steps if you are doing a dynamic version of the exercise. Continue to expand this time to your limits. Practice several times daily.

5. As you raise the tone from your lowest point to its highest level, visualize—or feel—the power rising from below your feet out through the top of your head. Each time you repeat the exercise, feel the power of the tone rise from below upward throughout the length of your whole body. Then on the next inhalation begin high and spiral the sound down to the lowest level. Spiral the sound up and down your body with each breath. The overall effect of the sound will be something akin to a siren. The time period of the actual transition from the highest to the lowest tone will be relatively short, usually about four seconds, with the end tone being held for however long is comfortable for you at that stage. Practice several times daily.

6. This step is very similar to the previous one, except here you repeatedly jump from the lowest to the highest tone of which you are capable without strain and without cracking your voice. Practice daily and often.

7. Again, this is the same as the one above, except you similarly jump from the highest to the lowest tone you are used to making. Practice daily and often.

8. Return to the pattern of step six and jump from the low tone to the high tone. In the performance of exercises six through eight, the duration of each of the tones will be about four to five seconds.

To follow correctly Marby's instructions, the runester should always follow steps one through eight in exactly the order given. In building up to a fully correct performance, you must master the first step before going on to the second. Each subsequent step is added to the repertoire after the previous one has been practiced for at least seven days. According to this schedule it should take at least 54 days to complete the program. When the program is complete, the runester will have a solid foundation in the art and practice of runic gymnastics and rune song.

At some point during this program, the runester should add basic mental affirmations to the routine. Each runester will be able to determine the best time for this addition. Some will have had sufficient training in basic concentration and visualization to not be distracted from the fundamental practice from the beginning, and so will be able to start with these affirmations quite soon. For those without much prior training, mastery of the fundamentals must precede these additions. For the I-rune the basic affirmation is the contemplation of the fact that your whole body is an "antenna"—a magnetic conductor of streams and currents from all five zones of the the cosmos. All of them flow to and through you, and all are running parallel to your own currents. You guide and channel them (see yourself in the midst of the whole cosmos) with the great distances of outer space and inner space above and below you.

According to Marby, the actual results of this program of exercises should be a feeling of overall vitality and strength, a feeling of lightness of being and rejuvenation of the soul, a feeling of being effective in action in all that you do, with clearer thoughts and quieter emotions. Furthermore, you ought to be able to increase your charisma—your ability to attract people to yourself—and to be able to settle strife between people in your immediate environment. You will become calm and vital, and will emit this quality into your surroundings.

The Working of Individual Runes

S.A. Kummer, in his book *Heilige Runenmacht*, taught a basic curriculum in the practice of individual runic postures in which the runester undertakes the work of individual runes in a certain unique order. According to Kummer's curriculum, this regimen will result in profound runic initiatory experiences, most of which he is unwilling to communicate in his book. My personal experiments carried out over a two-year period in the mid-1970s indicate that indeed there is much to what Kummer says, so I will simply present the exercises and let the runes speak for themselves!

Kummer's curriculum consists of a total of 13 runes, performed in the following order:

ᛁ ᚱ ᛉ ᚢ ᛏ ᛦ ᚺ ᛐ ᚲ ᛟ ᚠ ᚼ

IS KA MAN UR + NOT EH SIG TYR LAF OTHIL FA HAGAL

According to Kummer's way of thinking, the mystery of each rune is unlocked by the runester through practical exercise and experience of it, and then that rune opens the way to the rune that follows it. The sequence has an esoteric, Armanic significance that is revealed through practice.

According to the curriculum, each rune is to be practiced for a fortnight (14 days) before going on to the next rune. On average, the runester should be able to sustain the exercise for ten minutes, but he or she is urged to practice as often as possible. Although ultimately the sequence is constructed to form a powerful ritual of combined runic forces (as described in the latter part of this chapter and in chapter 10), each individual rune is to be mastered in its unique expression at this stage. Peculiar to Kummer's system is the inclusion of the cross posture between the U- and N-runes. This is really a non-runic holy sign of balance and synthesis—a posture bringing all of the gathered forces around the runester into a harmonious whole within the system of the magician. Until the time when this exercise is done, all the runic postures you have practiced in the curriculum should be practiced at least once a day. After that time period, you should take care to practice at least two or three of the other previously learned runic exercises for a few minutes each day. Mix the runes as you wish during these exercise periods. At least once a week you should run through the exercises in the sequence given up to the rune you are working on at the time. In these sessions it may seem that the runes are beginning to speak among themselves.

In the following illustrations of each of the runic postures (asanas) there is an indication of the flow of force patterns as the runic currents from the five zones (hardly discussed by Kummer himself) enter the body of the runester and/or are projected from the runester's body. Attention to these flow patterns and their direct experience is essential to success in rune yoga.

Because the orientation of the body for most of these exercises is to the north, the usual flow of force will be from the right (east) to the left (west). This may seem to run counter to the natural polarization of the body, in which the left is magnetic and draws power, while the right is electric and projects power. When facing east the body will be aligned in a more natural way, with the left to the magnetic north and the right to the electric south. The northward orientation provides greater *magical will*, which will aid the runester in actually feeling the conscious guidance of these forces rather than merely "going with the flow." These theories are virtually identical to those of Indian Tantric cosmology, with which the Teutonic cosmology shares a common ancestry.

For best results the runester is advised to practice as much as possible on the bare ground, with bare feet, in the open air. If you must work indoors, do so facing a window (open if possible). Further advice helpful to such practice is given in chapter 12, Steads of Rune Might.

IS If you have followed the instructions on the I-rune given above, the mystery of the rune should already be open to you. Nevertheless, practice it in the posture shown for 14 days. Use the mantra *iiiiisssss*, or simply *iiiiiii*. Practice drawing power from both above and below. When drawing force from below upwards, the runester sings the I-tone from a low pitch rising to a high one, as already discussed above. The opposite is done to draw power from above downward into the earth. The exercise is to be performed while facing magnetic north. The overall effects of the work, besides those expressed by Marby, are the strengthening of both the ego and consciousness of the unique indwelling self. This is the basis of self and of the work to come—the main-stave, or head-stave, of the working of rune yoga.

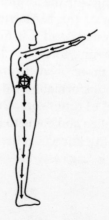

KA To perform the K-rune posture correctly, begin in the I-rune, and after some preliminary deep breathing exercises, lift your arms to a 45-degree angle out in front of you. You can also practice by using just the right or the left arm, leaving the other arm at your side. The palms should be facing out, aimed at the sun or moon. Sing the rune-name *KA*, and the formula *KA KE KI KO*

KU while visualizing the influx of force from the solar and lunar zones coursing through the palms to the solar plexus and being grounded into the earth zone. You should practice the K-rune facing eastward as well as northward. This exercise increases the overall abilities of the runester in every endeavor, but especially in the work of harnessing runic forces.

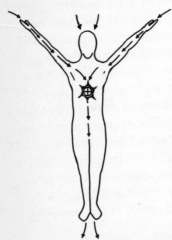

MAN Stand erect, and after some preliminary deep breaths in the I-rune posture, lift the arms out to the sides (slightly forward) at a 45-degree angle. Cup your palms upward to draw force from directly above. This force is also drawn in through the back of the head. The three lines of rune might converge in the thymus region and flow downward to be grounded. To effect this engagement, hum the sound *mmmmmmmmm*, alternating with the formula *MA ME MI MO MU*. The performance of the MAN-rune is among the most powerful in the system, and it is further discussed in chapter 14. In the MAN-rune, forces are drawn from all of the zones through these three "heavenly roots" into the runester, beginning the transformation into the god-man, which is the ultimate goal of rune work. During the course of this work, you will realize and come to know the power and character of this entity known as the god-man. Experiment with this exercise facing eastward as well as northward.

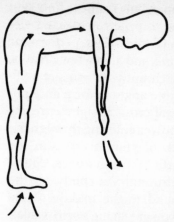

UR   Begin in the I-rune posture, and after seven deep breaths bend at the waist with fingers pointed straight down to the center of the earth—to the heart of the inner-earth zone. Remain in that posture for three breaths while singing or humming the *uuuuuuuuu* vocalic sound in a deep and sonorous manner. Here force is drawn from the depths of the inner-earth zone, circulated within the psychosomatic system concentrated in the solar plexus, and returned to the inner-earth zone through the fingertips. The whole exercise cycle of seven breaths in the I-rune posture and three in the U-rune while circulating subterranean streams should be repeated at least three times. At the conclusion of this portion of the exercise, lie down, back flat on the ground, head to magnetic north, and conduct deep breathing exercises in a comfortable rhythm. Visualize and feel yourself floating on the waves of telluric, subterranean streams of force. Drink deeply from the well of organic, regenerative force of eternal power.

The cross posture is not a rune proper, but is rather a holy sign used to balance collected elemental forces. First perform the I-rune, and after a few breaths, stretch out your arms at a 90-degree angle to form an equilateral cross. Imagine streams of power entering through the back of your head from the fourth and fifth zones, coursing through your body into the ground to the middle of the first zone. At the same time, as you are facing north, visualize the streams of atmospheric powers in the third (wave) zone coursing from east to west, through your right arm and out your left arm. Your heart is at the crossroads of a confluence of cosmic power. After this exercise has been practiced for seven or eight days, begin to turn in place in a clockwise direction. This is to be done with minimal movement in the feet: keep your knees together and let your feet do the work, turning to your right on the pivot of your right heel. The six rays of the wheel of the magical circle can act as the "stations" in this turning process. Skills learned here will intensify the power of other dynamic runic exercises, such as the HAGAL working that follows.

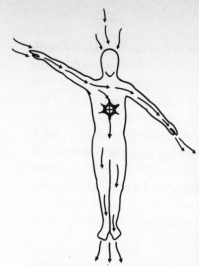

NOT After a few breaths in the basic I-rune posture, lift your arms to form the N-rune shape. Your right arm is at a 45-degree angle to the east, with the left arm forming a straight line with it to the west. Force is drawn through the right hand from the upper zones to the east and funneled down through the body, out the left arm into the ground and the inner-earth streams to the west. At the same time, force is drawn down through the length of the body from the back of the head. Where the two flows of force meet, in the region of the thymus gland (or heart chakra), a toroidal spiral of force begins that descends through the center of the body in a counterclockwise direction. Sing or hum the *nnnnnnnnn* sound or the vocalic formula *NA NE NI NO NU*. After the exercise, contemplation of problems will be likely to yield positive results.

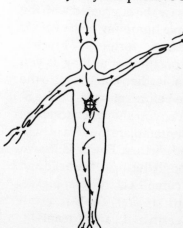

EH After a few breaths taken in the basic I-rune posture, and while facing northward, strike the E-rune posture as shown. This is the mirror image (and reverse polarity) of the N-rune. Here, as with the N-rune, the power is drawn from the right (east) and projected through the left (west). The flow of force with the E-rune is from below upward, just as with the N-rune it is from above downward (the force in the wave space in the atmosphere close to the earth usually flows from the east to the west). The runester must willfully draw force from the cosmic zone in through the back of the head and downward through the length of the body, otherwise there will be a natural tendency for the force to be drawn up from the inner-earth streams, which may not be conducive to achieving the purpose of this exercise—the attraction and holding of the ideal contrasexual mate. However, the runester may beneficially experiment with drawing force from below upward through the center of the body with the E-rune, which is the perfect reversal of the N-rune force.

SIG Begin with a few deep breaths in the I-rune posture, then squat down with your thighs and calves pressed together and your heels touching. Sing the name SIG (pronounced "zeeg") with a prolonged z and ee sound: zzzzeeeeeg. This can be alternated with the simple humming of the voiced zzzzzzzzzz formula. Practice the posture for as long as you are able, then come back to the I-rune posture to rest for a while before returning to the S-rune. During the entire operation, you should concentrate on the solar plexus region, and contemplate the idea of holiness, salvation, and success and victory. Power is drawn down from the cosmic zone through the top of the head and circulated in the psychosomatic complex at the solar plexus, then funneled into the inner-earth streams. The S-rune can also be used to draw on inner-earth and earth streams.

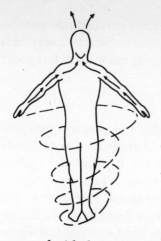

TYR After a few deep breaths in the I-rune posture, hold your arms out at a 45-degree angle from your body to form the T-rune posture as shown. Your palms should be pointed toward the earth, as power is drawn up in a spiraling fashion from the depths of the inner-earth and earth streams at a diameter equal to the distance between the centers of your palms. The spiraling force is engaged with the vocalic formula *TA TE TI TO TU*, or by simply humming in a low, sonorous tone while concentrating on the quality of the *T* sound. The power will spiral up around in a circle to the hands and then funnel upward and out through the head, as shown in the diagram. Through the power of this exercise the secrets of the earth and of its vast history can be unlocked, along with the records of previous incarnations of the individual runester.

LAF Following usual procedure, strike the L-rune posture by lifting both arms out in front of the body at a 45-degree angle. The fingers are pointed with the palms facing downward toward the ground. Power is drawn up from the depths of the inner earth and out through the arms in a pulsating pattern that rolls through and purifies the body, loading it with vital life force. Besides the rune name, the formulas *lllllllll* and *LA LE LI LO LU* can be used to engage this power. This rune increases overall vitality, and solidifies in a living way the progress made up to this point in the exercises.

OTHIL   To perform this posture correctly, stand with hands over head, palms flat against one another, and feet spread in line with the extension of the elbows. Feet should be flat on the ground, toes pointed slightly outward. Facing northward, and using the vocal formula *oooooooo*, draw earth streams up through the right foot into the body. The power rises to the region of the heart and is diverted up through the left arm and through the connection made between the palms into the right arm, where it descends through the body again and exits through the left foot back into the ground. This exercise circulates the power of the second (earth) zone in the field of the third (wave) zone, where it becomes a concrete antenna for the freely flowing odic forces in the atmosphere. The ring shaped by the arms forms an omni-directional receiver for the odic forces, and with practice the runester will become progressively more loaded with these powers, which protect and empower one to break through all bonds and barriers.

FA First assume the I-rune posture and take a few deep breaths. Then raise your arms to an approximate 45-degree angle, but with the left arm slightly higher than the right. Point your palms to the sun. Upon inhalation willfully draw the rays of the sun from the fourth (cosmic) zone and circulate the power within your body. (In order not to let the energy flow out into the ground, you may find it useful to lift the sole of one of your feet, probably the right, slightly off the ground upon inhalation.) On exhalation project the power back to the sun through your palms. You may also experiment using only one hand for reception and the other for projection. The vocalic formula to be used on exhalation is either *ffffffffff* or the fivefold *FA FE FI FO FU*. At least once a week this exercise should be done with the North Star. Experiments can also be carried out with other stars and heavenly bodies. With mastery of this rune, the magician begins to be able to project in effective and willed ways the powers he or she has been gaining.

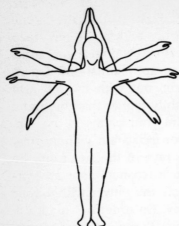

HAGAL   The final stage of this curriculum of initiation into the practice of runic yoga is the multifaceted practice of the crystalline HAGAL-rune. HAGAL is the synthesis of the collective rune might. In order to be most effectively performed, the complex HAGAL exercise must be done in a complete thought vacuum. HAGAL is the form of all thought, or intellect, and therefore cannot correctly be limited to any one particular thought. The exercise is done in four stages: (1) cross-posture preliminary exercise, (2) combination of N- and E-runes, (3) combination of I-, M-, and T-runes, and (4) a cross-posture closing. The first and last parts are identical. Perform the cross posture while turning in a clockwise direction singing the formula *ha ha ha ha ha ha*. This can also be done by simply humming in a deep, sonorous way while imagining the sound of either *h* or the repeated *ha* formula. This, and all the other parts of the exercise, should begin and end in the north or east. The second phase of the exercise is done by turning in the circle while performing the N-rune posture and mantra, then the cross posture, followed by the N-rune posture and mantra, and concluded by another performance of the cross posture. The third phase is done by performing the I-rune posture, then the cross posture, then the M-rune posture followed by the connective cross posture, and concluding with the T-rune exercise. The fourth and final phase is a repetition of the first. After one cycle of this exercise, the runester will have turned in position a total of eleven times. Remember to keep your movements flowing and smooth while doing these dynamic exercises. To summarize the complex HAGAL exercise:

1)   +

2) ᚼ + ᚠ +

3) ᛁ + ᛉ + ᛏ

4)   +

Rune-Yogic Rituals

The curriculum of rune-yogic exercises outlined in detail above is really a single, vast rune-yogic rite, but beyond this, the individual runester can also create unique rune-yogic rituals for specific purposes. Once the runic gateways are opened, the individual runester will not only know how to engage these forces effectively but will also be informed about which runes to use to gain the desired result. In reality there is no simple recipe-book approach to this aspect—experience is the best teacher.

The runes are keys that unlock the doors connecting the realm of ideas to the realm of things. The key to unlocking the runes themselves is found in their sounds and shapes. This secret is so simple, yet so profound, that it is usually lost by those expecting anything else. If the runester has faithfully undergone the complete curriculum of the 13 runes, he or she will have gained the secret of rune might on a first-hand basis. It is, of course, recommended that you become familiar with all parts of this book before undertaking the curriculum, and that you incorporate as much of its wisdom into your work as is possible for you at this time.

Formula of Engagement

A daily form of rune-yogic exercise that can be performed to engage the runic forces completely and quickly is the threefold formula *I-U-M (Z)*. This can also serve as a model for the construction of further rites of this kind. To perform this formula of engagement, first take up the I-rune posture, and after a few preliminary breaths begin to sing the I-rune sound formula (*iiiiiiiii* and/or *iiiiiiizzzzzzzz*). When the feeling of engagement between the zones above and the zones below has been established through the vertical column of the runester, speak *dynamically* (see chapter 8 on the topic of dynamic speech) the following words: "Self-knowing, I am a staff for beams and waves of rune might!" Now smoothly shift into the U-rune posture by bending at the waist, with the fingers pointed to the ground— feel the rune might gathered in the upper part of your body flow out through your fingers back into the ground, and beginning a circulation of power drawn through your feet, continue the circulatory pattern. Sing the sound formula of the U-rune (*uuuuuuuuu* and/or the rune name *uuuuurrrrr*). Do this three or four times before dynamically speaking, "Self-knowing, I shape the might from the deepest depths, out of the realm of the earth, out of the realm deep below." In doing this, be sure to engage both the earth streams and the subterranean inner-earth streams. Now swiftly but smoothly straighten back up and raise your arms to the M-rune (elder Z-rune) posture. Feel the sudden engagement of the forces of the higher zones as you sing the sound formula *mmmmmmmmm* (or *zzzzzzzzz*). The first few times you do this rite, repeat the whole cycle until you feel the power begin to lessen from one repetition to another. In this way you will see what it feels like for rune might to increase and decrease in you, and you can gauge further successes more accurately. The more these rites are done, the more rune might is built up in a permanent way in the fiber of your being.

Rune-Yogic Rite of Success

This is an example of a complex rite that takes into account almost all of the factors discussed in this book. Again, it can be used as a model for the construction of further individualized workings. For this rite we are indebted to the work of Karl Spiesberger.

1. Perform the preliminary I-rune posture and song (*iiiiiiii*) until the rune might is felt to be engaged, then repeat a dynamic mantra that will engage your will with the will of your higher power. (This is really best done on an individual basis, but one of the forms suggested by Spiesberger is "Vibrating in the primal field of force, I am one with its will.")

2. Take up the T-rune posture and dynamically say, "Tyr-Tyr, Tyr-Tyr, Tyr-Tyr! Might waxes, well-being spreads, and luck increases—the fruit of the fight: Victory!" (G. *Sieg!*)

3. When the word "Victory" (*Sieg*) is spoken, shift into the Sig-Tyr posture and feel the rune might vibrate from an epicenter around your heart with the circumference of the field at your palms. The centers in the forehead and genitals are also engaged, as shown in the illustration below.

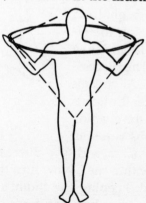

The Sig-Tyr Posture

Now sing the formula "sig-tyr" at least three times, but you may continue until the vibratory field has been activated.

4. Next form the hand posture of the S-rune in front of the body at about eye level. When this is done, dynamically say, "The might in me is victorious!" When this is said, you should feel an oscillation of power between the heart center and the S-rune formed by the hands.

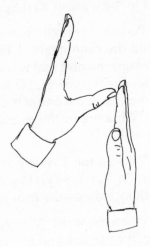

5. Now smoothly shift your hands overhead to form the H-rune hand posture. The palms of the hands are to face each other. At this point there is a new influx of rune might from the upper zones. Sing the H-rune sound formula, and then dynamically say, "The success-bringing force of the All streams into me!" Now lower the hands to the point where the meeting point of the thumbs is just in front of the heart chakra, and say, "Success-bringing force of the All works within me!" Now turn the palms so that they face outward, keeping the thumbs touching at all times, and say, "Success-bringing force of the All works through me!"

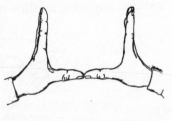

6. Draw the left hand in to your solar plexus and lay the palm flat on that center—feel the power stream from the center of your being through your left arm and around and out through your right arm. As the power flows out, trace the H-rune in front of you in this form:

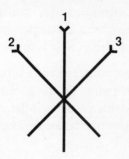

In doing this, simply imagine the rune being drawn in space before you at a distance of three or four feet as the rune might is flowing out the fingers of your right hand. This gives an objective projection of your collected rune might centering on the success-bringing forces.

7. Now grip both shoulders in the elder M-rune or D-rune posture (ᛗ) and softly sing the sound formula: *mmmaaannn.*

8. Next, silently quiet your mind with the thoughts Quiet-Stillness-Silence. Remain in the ᛗ posture through the ninth step.

9. If you have a specific desire for success in a given task or situation, you should now visualize that success taking place in the objective world. If you are interested in causing internal changes within your own subjective world (e.g., breaking bad habits, gaining confidence), then repeat a specially constructed dynamic suggestion, or visualize

scenes of how your life will be once the transformation has taken place. This is the real *working* segment of the rite in which the powers gathered previously are wielded according to the personal will of the runester.

10. Release the ᛗ posture, slowly let your arms fall to your sides in the I-rune posture, and dynamically say or think, "Holy rune might leads me to my hidden goal!" At this point *realize* that the goal is already reached.

11. Finally, the excess collected rune force is to be "grounded" by placing your palms on the ground and perhaps by resting for a while with your back flat on the ground and your head toward the north (as always).

Chapter 8

Rune Mantras

The whole topic of rune mantras, or rune singing, has actually been introduced in a basic way in chapter 7. There is, however, much that can be learned from a technical standpoint that will vastly improve the effectiveness of any rune work. Because the rune as such is an immaterial mystery, and the various material reflections of it are actually *symbolic* keys of its reality, all facets of these symbolic keys need to be taken into account when unlocking the doors to true rune might. A symbol is not just an arbitrary sign standing for something else; rather, it is an actual reflection, or even fragment, of a real quality or structure. The runes are actually multidimensional keys, and they must be evoked in more dimensions than just the three normally at our disposal. Through a conscious combination of the various runic qualities of form, sound, and number, together with other pieces of lore presented here and elsewhere, the mysteries can be unlocked and used.

Rune songs (mantras) are most usually used in conjunction with the performance of rune postures (asanas), as demonstrated in chapter 7. This combination of form and sound is a powerful key to rune might. However, rune mantra can also be combined with other ways of evoking rune forms—for example, with rune signing (tracing the runes in the air), rune thinking (visualizing the runes in the mind), or rune carving (actually carving the rune forms into wood, the earth, stone, etc.).

The mantric practices presented here can be combined with any other magical form-evoking technique, or they can be used alone, since the *sound* itself has a form of its own as it vibrates in the atmospheric wave space.

The Knowledge of Breath

It is very important to have conscious control over your breathing patterns or rhythms in the performance of runic mantras. The most important thing to remember when learning breath control is to maximize your intake (and outflow) of breath, and to do it in a *regular* and *conscious* way. Various schools of this science, whether traditional Indian pranayama or others, will insist on certain formulaic rhythms. These may have intrinsic powers for some, but what is primary in importance is that the rhythm be suited to *your* psycho-physical makeup.

General guidelines that would be good for all to follow are (1) that the breath be a *full* one, completely filling and emptying the lungs, and (2) that the rhythm be a regular one. To ensure a full breath, follow this procedure: First depress your diaphragm, filling the bottom of your lungs; then expand the rib cage, filling the main body of the lungs; and finally, lift the shoulders and collarbone, filling the very top part of the lungs. This is the full cycle of breath that will ensure a maximum intake of breath. On exhalation, reverse the process. This may take some practice to get used to at first, and so it should be the object of exercise in its own right for a time. This will improve concentration on breath and pave the way for more intense rune work. The actual rhythm you use—that is, the ratio between the time spent inhaling, holding the breath in, exhaling, and letting the breath out—must be consciously controlled in order to be maximally effective. In his book *Runenmagie*, Karl Spiesberger suggests experimentation with the following rhythms:

1) 5 seconds inhale
   1 second hold
   5 seconds exhale
   (Wait for the physical urge to inhale before beginning the next cycle.)

2) 4 seconds inhale
   2 seconds hold
   4 seconds exhale
   2 seconds hold

3) 5 seconds inhale
   3 seconds hold
   7 seconds exhale
   3 seconds hold

Of course, the longer period of exhalation is primarily due to the need for relatively more time in which to perform the mantras themselves. Therefore, it is often found that breathing exercises done for their own sake may have slightly different rhythms from those done in conjunction with mantras. The best way to time the seconds may be with the heartbeat, or perhaps a metronome could be used.

Building of Rune Mantras

In the German school of rune magic certain aspects of the mantric system are derived from the mystical analysis of language revealed in the studies of Guido von List, some are rooted in S.A. Kummer's studies of the esoteric basis of the sound patterns in traditional yodling (also spelled *yodel-ing*), while others are derived from the theories of F.B. Marby (e.g., "dynamic speech"). Here we will explore some of these theoretical and practical aspects.

First the basic simple sound value of the rune can usually be used as a mantra in itself. This is true for all the vowel sounds *a, e, i, o, u* and for all the sounds that can be made with a continuous stream of breath: *f, th, r, h, n, s, l, m.* The basic magical utility of each of these can be found in the Armanic runic table in chapter 6. Certain other consonantal runic sounds cannot be made in a continuous stream of breath, such as the sounds *k, t, b, g.* These must be combined with a vowel in order to make them pronounceable. (Kummer also suggests that the runester can hum—that is, vibrate the vocal chords and *imagine* the sound of these runes repeated continuously.) As each vowel sound gives the consonantal sound an added quality, all five vowel sounds must be repeated with the consonant in order to give it a qualitative balance in favor of the consonant. If the sound *KA,* a combination of *K* and *A,* is repeated, then you will have created a balance in which *K* is no more powerful in your mantra than *A.* On the other hand, *KA-KE-KI-KO-KU* has *K* five times and only one each of the vowels, thus placing primary emphasis on the general power of the *K*-sound.

The syllabic combinations are also practiced with the other consonants as well. These simple "kernel" words, such as *FA, FE, FI, FO,* or *FU,* represent combinations (sonic bind-runes) of the qualities inherent in the individual runic sounds.

Key to the Mystery Language
According to Guido von List

In the last work published during his lifetime, *Die Ursprache der Ario-Germanen und ihre Mysteriensprache* (The Primal Language of the Aryo-Germanic People and their Mystery Language), List laid out his esoteric theories on the hidden meanings of sound. His system is in many ways similar to Kabbalism, but instead of depending on numerical values to unlock the secret meanings of language, phonetic values are used. It is a sort of sonic Kabbalah. The key to the system is contained in Table 8.1. This table is a somewhat simplified version of one presented in List's book. Since there is inherent runic power in the sounds themselves, the system can be used for any Germanic language, ancient or modern, and only slight modifications need be made to convert the system from German to English.

In the Listian system, the consonant-vowel combinations such as *FA, FE, FI, FO, FU* are called *bud* words, or *kernel* words. There are ten kernel consonants as shown, and five kernel vowels. Note that *TH* and *D* are esoterically equivalent, as are *B* and *P*. It is unimportant whether the ordering of the sounds comes vowel-consonant or consonant-vowel; the power and meaning is in the combination of sound qualities, not in their ordering. These kernel words can then be combined to form *Ur* words, or primeval words. A third kind of word is the *root* word. A root word may be the same as an Ur word or even a kernel word. The rune names themselves are all considered root words. From the standpoint of the operative rune magician, it is most important to be able to construct magical sound formulas from this system by synthesizing the esoteric qualities indicated in the table. List himself only published the passive uses of the system, as a method of esoterically analyzing the hidden meanings of language—*kala*.

As an example, we could take the word *Odin* (=od-in) and analyze it according to the data in Table 8.1. There we see that *od* indicates an ordered material manifestation of the primal aether, and *in* is the spiritual order of primal water. By understanding the synthesis of these qualities, we learn an esoteric meaning of the name: The one that manifests aetheric power ruled over by the spiritual order of formation. The table can be used to unlock any word or name according to the Listian system, but it can also be used to create powerful runic mantras, or to make existing mantras more deeply conscious and magically effective.

The esoteric meanings of the consonants are most evident from the Armanic runic table presented in chapter 6, as well as from the Listian analysis of their elemental qualities as presented in Table 8.1. It is with the vowels that the most complexity of understanding arises, and therefore we will delve a bit deeper into their meanings here. When spoken, chanted, or sung, these esoteric qualities should be evoked as strongly as possible in the mind of the runester.

Rune Might

Table 8.1
Key to Listian Mystery Language

		I — primal fire, cause or power	II — primal air, desire, will	III — primal earth, ability, art, magic	IV — primal ether, the act	V — primal water, law, law of nature	VI — heavenly fire order	VII — heavenly fire order in spiritual interior	VIII — midgard order in material exterior	IX — all-light forming traits	X — moon completion
1-4	1. cause or power 2. desire or will 3. ability, art, magic 4. the act	A									
		FA	RA	KA ga	ThA da	NA	SA	TA	BA pa	LA	MA
5-6	5. law, law of nature 6. order	E	FE	RE	KE ge	ThE de	NE	SE	TE	BE pe	LE	ME
7	7. spiritual order	I	FI	RI	KI gi	ThI di	NI	SI	TI	BI pi	LI	MI
8-9	8. material order 9. forming traits	O	FO	RO	KO go	ThO do	NO	SO	TO	BO po	LO	MO
10	10. completion	U	FU	RU	KU gu	ThU du	NU	SU	TU	BU pu	LU	MU
1-4	1. cause or power 2. desire or will 3. ability, art, magic 4. the act	A	AF	AR	AK ag	ATh ad	AN	AS	AT	AB up	AL	AM
5-6	5. law, law of nature 6. order	E	EF	ER	EK eg	ETh ed	EN	ES	ET	EB ep	EL	EM
7	7. spiritual order	I	IF	IR	IK ig	ITh id	IN	IS	IT	IB ep	IL	IM
8-9	8. material order 9. forming traits	O	OF	OR	OK og	OTh od	ON	OS	OT	OB op	OL	OM
10	10. completion	U	UF	UR	UK ug	UTh ud	UN	US	UT	UB up	UL	UM

The Esoteric Meaning of the Runic Vowels
According to Guido von List

A is the divine power in threefoldedness, and its expression is pure force or energy in the cosmos. It is articulated in the following complex way:

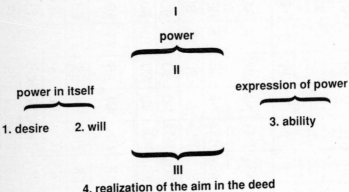

E is the LAW according to which power or force has its *orderly* effect on its aim. It is the effect of the three stages of development on the world of the four elements. *E* expresses the cosmic function of the law of seven (3 + 4), which is the law of the natural order of the cosmos.

I expresses the value or quality of the divine threefold power as a UNITY. It is the unifying force making things whole, holding them together, forming a foundation for positive, energetic development. *I* provides the "spiritual order" as a foundation for further evolution.

O is order made manifest in the particulars of physical reality. The power of *O* is the formative element in the physical manifestation of individual characteristics or traits.

U expresses the completion or perfection of the impetus of the divine power made whole with its manifestation in the cosmos—this is the law of assimilation in the All.

To gain a more complete understanding of List's cosmology, the runester can consult List's *The Secret of the Runes* and the introductory remarks to that work. Another aspect of Listian *kala*, which is too complex to discuss here, but which nevertheless cannot go unmentioned, is the idea that each of these kernel words undergoes a three-leveled interpretation according to the cyclical law of Arising, Becoming, Passing Away to New Arising—or Birth, Life, Death/Rebirth. Each kernel word can be interpreted as expressing a generative aspect of the quality in question, or an evolutionary/manifested one, or one indicative of a destructive or waning aspect. The key to which meaning is involved is most probably contained in the exoteric meaning of the word.

For our purposes only, the Listian system should only be used to construct powerful magical mantras in a systematic way. An example of one of these used by the Armanen themselves is constructed from the five root words of the vowels:

AR-EH-IS-OS-UR

As the vowel sounds express the spectrum of manifestation, this holy mantric word is the magical key to the realization of this manifestation in the practicing rune magician. The consonantal sounds also give specific nuances of meaning to this sonic manifestation of cosmic wholeness.

Let us say the runester would like to develop skills in art or magic and have these skills guided by spiritual principles. To this end a complex mantra might be created:

KA-SI-IT-BO-LU-AK

This, of course, works on the same principle as sigil magic, in which bind-runes are created to form a visual talismanic image that acts as a focus for magical intention. Here we are creating a coherent audible or sonic magical formula for the same purpose. In fact, a visual bind-rune such as the one below could be created to act as a visual focus for a sonic working of this kind.

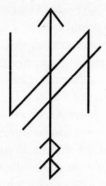

Another method of constructing runic mantras is to take a mantric affirmation in natural language (for example, modern English) and transform it into an esoteric magical language. This can be done in two ways. The simple mantric affirmation *I am rich* is first turned into the esoteric mantra *I-AM-RI-IK*. Now, the magician can either chant the magical mantric version (pronounced "ee-ahm-ree-eek") or simply repeat the exoteric, natural "I am rich" while concentrating on the underlying esoteric key to the sounds. It can be seen that this exercise has many things in common with, for example, the technique of "sigilization" used by Austin Osman Spare, which is really more or less identical with the ancient runic practice of creating magical bind-runes from names, words, or whole phrases. For magical efficiency it is important that the words and names involved be removed at least one step, but preferably more, from the natural expression. If the runester were to make the mantric affirmation "I am rich" into a bind-rune to supplement the sonic power of the mantra, he or she would simply take the phrase, turn it into runic equivalents:

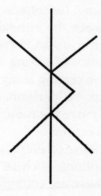

and combine these runes in a single glyph:

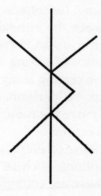

This glyph has now become a visual esoteric reflection of the sonic version.

Rune Yodling

Yodling is a unique form of vocalic practice now best known as a feature of Alpine folklore. It is thought to have been an ancient mode of long-distance communication through the peaks and valleys of the vast region of the central European Alps. The magicians of the Armanen school hold that these are actually ancient sacred mantric formulas that have been preserved in the isolated, culturally conservative regions of the high Alps. These vocal formulas continued to be practiced by traditional people, like so much else in folklore, long after the sacred importance had been forgotten.

Yodles are vocal formulas in what appears to be a non-sensical language—simply melodic combinations of consonant and vowel sounds. In other words, they are constructed in ways very similar to the ways runic mantras are created, and in fact traditional yodles are believed to be vocal or sonic versions of old invocations to runic forces. The essence of what is meant by yodling is, however, in the *way* the sounds are sung. Essentially yodling is a modulation of the voice between the normal chest singing and a falsetto centered in the throat and head region. This is, after all, the essential practice of raising and lowering the vibratory centers of rune singing along the axis of the body. Any runic mantra can be performed in this manner to increase its power to move the runic forces along the central axis of the bodily centers.

The scientific runological literature is full of references to "nonsense" inscriptions, such as *LUWATUWA* on the Vadstena *brakteate*. These are certainly runic mantras that could have been performed in a yodling fashion. Non-Germanic observers of the ancient Teutonic style of vocal performance always compared much of what they heard to the barking of dogs, or to the cackling of hens. All of this most probably referred to magical incantations and war chants, etc., sung vigorously in the rising and falling tones characteristic of the yodle—something quite shocking to the ear unaccustomed to it. It might also be pointed out that the Germanic term for magical incantation, *galdr*, is derived from a word describing the croaking sound that a crow or raven makes. On page 91 are reproductions with musical notation of traditional yodles, which were suggested by S.A. Kummer as models for further runic work. Kummer also points out that the magical effect will be increased if the yodling is performed in the corresponding rune postures (or in the MAN-posture), and ideally they are to be performed in an echoing valley where their power can be magnified. In a profane sense the yodles reverberate over valleys and peaks and can effect communication over many miles; but in a magical sense they reverberate over the depths and heights of existence and can effect communication throughout the worlds.

Traditional Yodles

Remember, *j* is pronounced as an English *y*, and the letter *å* is sounded like the combination "aw" and "ä" sounds (like the long English *a*).

1. From St. Radegrund am Schöckl near Graz; Stiermark.

2. From Alt-Aussee, Stiermark. Received from the Forester Gruber on the Mondsee.

3. From Fuchsl, Salzburg (1888).

Já di ri di já i ti ri di ri ti ri ti ti

já di ri di já i ti ri di ri ti ti

4. Yells. Calls from the Offensee collected 1886.

1. I juch!

2. Ju ju ju ju ju!

3. I já de rå!

4. Ju hu hu!

5. Ju hu hu hu hu!

6. I u hu!

7. I ju hu hu hu!

Marby's Dynamic Speech

F. B. Marby developed his own theories concerning the use of sound in the practice of runic exercises. Writing in volume 5/6 of his *Marby-Runen-Bücherei* (p. 113) he said:

> All phenomena and expressions are based in their origins on electrical valences and their interplay. The dynamism of this interplay brings into being all processes, all living phenomena. Also the speaking of certain sounds must always accordingly represent a dynamic process, a transformation of electrical valences in sound, or a transformation of sounds in electrical valences, and following from this a transformation of so-called material substance as well. Speech is an un-fold-ing of forces which can propel, transform, build up, or break things down.

Marby posited that the interior of the mouth could be used as a magical vibratory instrument—a sort of microcosmic magical chamber in which the modulations made in the sounds could and would have their effects on the interior and exterior worlds, if energized by the will and imagination of the runester. In this he was only following ideas laid down centuries before by early Indian yogis. For example, at least one traditional school of Indian mysticism teaches that the correct performance of the sacred mantric syllable "om," or "aum," is keyed to the idea that it expresses in vocal terms the emergence of substance from the depths of being (visualized as the back of the throat where the sound starts) to the outermost reaches of manifestation (visualized as the closed lips where the sound ends). Thus, vibrating from the back of the throat to the limits of the lips is the microcosmic, magical correspondent to vibrating throughout the whole macrocosm—it is a reenactment of the creative process of the *vac* (the creative magical voice, or word, of Brahman).

In Marby's system, which can be integrated with that of List, the vowels are the basic sounds of creation and manifestation, while the consonants are seen as qualifying limitations, or borders, of the pure vocalic vibrations. Marby identified the vocalic sounds within vibratory bands in the human aura. Figure 8.1 represents a simplified diagram of these bands (the original German includes the non-English sounds "ö" and "ü," which are not used as basic sounds by other runesters anyway). The "i" sound has the most dense vibratory rate and is therefore closest to the body, and interacts most directly with the body; the "a" sound has the highest vibratory rate and actually reaches out into the farthest realms. This or some other form of "onionskin" visualization of the energy fields around the human physical vehicle can be used to intensify the practice of mantras by *seeing* and *feeling* the corresponding sounds vibrating

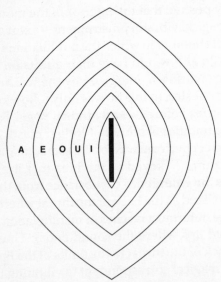

Figure 8.1 The Vocalic Bands of Force
according to F.B. Marby

and energizing the various fields of force. Also, this model can be used to intensify the experience of runic asanas, as the runester *feels* the connection of various centers (chakras) in the limbs as they make contact with the different levels of energy fields. Once these or similar bands of force are strongly visualized around the body, the hands can be placed within them to effect a withdrawal of force from that particular band, channeling it to other parts of the internal or external sphere.

Chapter 9

Group Rune Rituals

T he practice of rune yoga, or runic gymnastics, as outlined in the previous two chapters, can be greatly intensified by increasing the number of people involved in generating the field of runic forces. Any rite or exercise that can be done alone can be done in concert with others, thereby increasing the overall effect of the exercise. The combined presence of runesters striking the rune postures will draw a maelstrom of runic forces to the place of power, and the collective singing or chanting of the rune mantras will create a sphere of resounding rune might harmonious to the aims of the exercise or rite. Here we are only really talking about increasing the *quantity* of the available rune force at the disposal of the gathered runesters. There may or may not be some transformation in the essential *quality* of the evoked force. However, certain group practices, which we will discuss in some detail here, are specifically meant to transform the quality of the rune force. No matter if you have practiced the rune long and hard on your own with good results, you will find that in the practice of certain of these combined rune postures and exercises, a wholly new dimension of the power of the rune will be opened to your direct experience.

In the theory of the German runic tradition, the reason for this increase in power and qualitative experience is that the two or more runesters taking part in the exercise usually act as positive and negative poles in a pattern similar to that found in electromagnetic phenomena. This quality is most evident when the gender of the runesters doing the group work is divided (preferably equally) between men and women. Just as certain shapes or formations in the environment are thought to have innate qualities of power, so too are the genders of the practitioners believed to have influence in runic exercises.

It is best if the individual runesters have already done basic work in rune yoga before attempting the combined versions of these runes. The reason for this is that the individual ought to have solid experience of how the forces flow within him/herself before attempting to share them with someone else. It is just a matter of increasing the chances for a powerful and successful working.

Exercises for Two Runesters

Almost all of the runes can be performed in combined versions. Those with two "head" staves, such as ᛉ , ᛟ , or ᚺ , are ideal for this, but as the examples demonstrated below indicate, all the others could also be performed in a combined fashion.

In all other respects, other than the particulars of the actual formation of the combined postures, the criteria for the correct performance of these runic exercises are the same as those for the corresponding single runes. The rune songs are to be sung and the visualizations undertaken as before. The exact flows of runic force may in some instances vary from the ways they flow in the single version, however. In this, direct experience is the best teacher.

The MAN-rune can be combined in at least two significant ways. The two runesters can stand side by side in the MAN-rune posture, with the palms of their right and left hands respectively touching the crown of his or her partner's head as shown.

Or, the two partners can stand facing one another, each touching the other's forehead (third eye); or similarly, while facing each other the two partners can touch the other's hipbone or solar plexus with the right or left palm. This exercise can have the special nuance of binding the partners together in a magically powerful relationship.

The combined performance of the MAN-rune can also be used as a mode of initiatory "passing of power" from one runester to another.

The HAGAL rune in its older form N can be formed by the two partners facing one another and grasping the upper arms of his or her partner so that the form of the H-rune is imitated.

The older D-rune $\bowtie$ (called DAG in the German tradition) can be formed with two partners standing next to each other performing the THORN-rune posture with their elbows touching. One partner practices with the right arm, the other, with the left arm.

Sexual Practices for Two Runesters

It is in the area of contra-sexual practices that the power of the runes can be most increased. The most general and widely practiced of these simply involve a man and a woman performing the rune postures while in close physical contact. Remember that any bind-rune combination *can* be intensified in power through performance with a member of the opposite sex. The performance of any of the MAN-rune exercises above in this manner are good starting points.

The usual basic rites of a contra-sexual nature are the combined exercise of the HAGAL- and the GIBOR-runes. To perform the combined GIBOR-rune, the two partners stand facing each other in close physical contact with each bodily center pressing close to that of the partner. The posture of the G-rune is taken up (a standing spread-eagle), with the palms touching and the feet pointed outward and aligned with one another. The GIBOR is the rune of dynamic, magical combination of sexual energies, so this exercise is best suited to this rune. Similarly, the HAGAL-rune may be struck as a combination of the E- and N-runes. Again the partners should face one another, with the female partner in the N-rune posture and the male in the E-rune posture. Practice both with the hands clasped together and the fingers pointed in the way these runes are normally practiced. This exercise promotes the collective increase in power between the two partners.

The combined performance of the E-rune in the older form M is a powerful symbol of the mystery of the wedding of two persons under the traditional law of the folk. This is performed to strengthen the bonds of love between a man and a woman. To perform it, the two partners stand face to face and simply reach out and grasp each others' hands in imitation of the M -rune as shown. This can also be practiced by just touching fingertips.

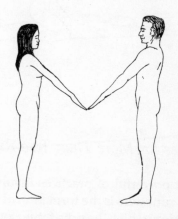

The practices discussed up to this point are sexual in nature, to be sure, and have as their cornerstone the alternation of sexual current between a man and a woman, but there is nothing of a necessarily overt genital-erotic nature in them. Such practices do exist, however. Obviously these practices can only be effectively undertaken by persons with a strong magico-erotic relationship. The double-THORN or DAG-rune can be performed in this way by both partners facing one another and using their hands to stimulate the erotic center of the other.

Actual runic positions for sexual intercourse have been suggested also. For example, for the K-rune, the female partner is in a kneeling position over the male, who is lying stretched out with his hands overhead as shown below. These practices were first published in a public forum in Josef Bienert's book *Raunende Runen* (1964).

Exercises for More Than Two Runesters

The most powerful of practices involving groups of three or more runesters is the formation of huge chains or rings of power into which the rune force can be evoked, circulated and increased, and then projected to do magical work of some kind. This kind of rite is often used for healing purposes, in which case the person to be treated is brought into the current of combined runic forces to effect a revivification, rejuvenation, and rebalancing of his or her psychosomatic field.

Runes commonly used in group work are the MAN- and TYR-runes. These can be performed in geometrical configurations (three runesters forming a triangle, four a square, etc.); or in larger groups (six or more), a true ring or circle can more easily be envisioned and used. The point of contact between the runesters can be the lightest touching of the fingertips, the pressing of palm to palm, or the firm clasping of hands. The important thing is that the group find a method that works best for them and that they practice the passing of rune force through this ring until they are comfortable with their ability to work together. The current should be visualized (most often in a red or a rose-hued light), but more importantly, *felt*, as it courses through the arms of the runesters and passes from one hand to the other. This can have the general effect of strengthening the feelings of magical bonding among the members of your runic circle; or, once the rune force is built up to a high level of intensity, it can be released to do some external magical task. The use of the runic circle in works of healing will be discussed in chapter 13.

Sexual Practices for More Than Two Runesters

When possible, the construction of runic chains or rings should alternate between male and female members of the circle. The exercises with contra-sexual importance mentioned in the section above can also be intensified if the two partners doing the exercise are in secondary contact with two others doing the same exercise or one complementary to it. For example, a male runester and a female runester could be doing the G-rune exercise as outlined above while two others are doing the same thing, only the feet and hands of the other pair are lightly touching those of the first pair. This could then be built into a whole ring of many runesters. More overtly erotic practices include combined sexual positions, such as the one illustrated on page 104 for the performance of the F-rune. A male lies stretched out while two female runesters kneel over him—one over his sexual regions (engaged in sexual intercourse) and the other over his mouth (engaged in cunnilingus). The magical utility of such exercises may be limited except for those already trained in the ways and means of sexual magic; but at any stage of development it looks like an interesting end *an sich.*

Chapter 10

Rune Dance

The practice of putting the various runic postures in motion, of making them "dynamic," was probably introduced by F.B. Marby. But it was S.A. Kummer who really developed it extensively. In his *Heilige Runenmacht* he wrote: "Among our forebears, the holy, religious, Germanic dance was the dance of the initiates, the priests and priestesses, who received especially high cosmic waves by means of this dancing and thereby developed their innermost kernel-essence, their divine 'I,' to its highest unfoldment, and got high inspiration, spiritual abilities, clairvoyance, etc."

Kummer maintains that the initiated dance of the ancient rune magicians was free of what he refers to as "ape-like movements." He would characterize the initiated dance of the Teutons as something in which only calm, harmony, and rhythm prevailed. It must be made clear, however, that there probably was more than one school of sacred or magical dance in the Teutonic cultural sphere in ancient times, and that at least one of them, that of Freya, was characterized by somewhat "wilder" forms, of which S.A. Kummer might not have approved! But as the runester can see, these "dances" are really more akin to dynamic yogic exercises, the dance of the Sufis, or the Gurdjieff movements than anything we might ordinarily associate with dancing now. Kummer is at pains, as he was when discussing the origins of yodeling and how it was preserved, to point out that some of the basic movements of dynamic rune exercises have often been preserved in traditional forms of Germanic folk dancing.

These exercises are best performed outdoors on a level surface. For most of them a good deal of room is needed: a surface area of about seven to ten yards in diameter would be ideal. Kummer also said that these dances were usually performed naked, except where the initiates of what he calls the priesthood were involved. They were supposed to have worn robes fitted with jewels corresponding to the magical purpose at hand.

First Dance

Standing in the south of a circle seven to nine yards in diameter, take up the MAN-rune posture after performing a few preliminary breathing exercises. Now begin to move with relatively short side steps to your left (i.e., in a clockwise direction), always facing toward the center of the circle. During this whole phase of the exercise the sound *mmmmmm* should be sung or hummed. As you return to the southernmost point of the circle, begin to spiral ever inward to the center of the circle on each successive turn, until you are standing in the center. Once the center has been reached, begin to spin in the middle of the ring while more intensely humming the *mmmmmm* sound and while intensely concentrating on the solar plexus region. The turning should be made to be progressively faster. After a high level of concentration has been attained in the sound of the M-rune, the student should slip into silence, entering a complete thought vacuum. If thoughts should begin to creep into the mind, resume the humming to eliminate them. After some time in the thought vacuum, lie down in restful contemplation. In the state of mind that falls on the runester after these rune dances, there often come flashes of inspiration, insight, and understanding. This period of rest should follow all rune-dance exercises.

This exercise should not be repeated more than three times a day. It is also recommended that the TYR-rune be performed in the same way. This exercise should be experimented with by turning in both a clockwise and a counterclockwise direction. An alternate mode of doing the exercise would be to begin turning in the middle in a clockwise direction, working your way *outward*, then turn back *inward* in a counterclockwise direction. This is especially recommended for the TYR-rune dance.

Second Dance

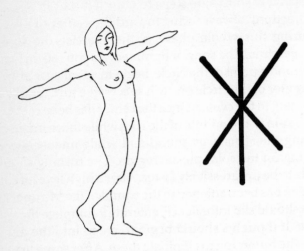

In the basic cross posture, with the palms facing upward, begin a basic waltz-step in a circle while singing the "ha" sound in a rhythmic fashion. Concentration should be maintained on the solar plexus *and* on the third eye, or pineal gland. After the H-rune has been thoroughly invoked, you should lapse into a perfect thought vacuum while gently swaying in the center of the circle. If thoughts should begin to arise in the mind, again begin the waltz-step and the singing of the "ha" sound.

Third Dance

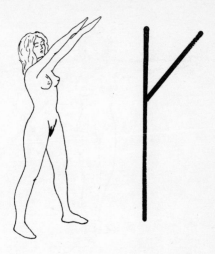

Start in the static form of the K-rune exercise. Take three side steps to the left and then three side steps back to the right, the whole time evoking the negative state within the mind. Do this cycle of movements about seven times before resting. Kummer advises the runester to undertake this exercise at the time of the waning moon, and to do it in a time and place where the student will go unobserved.

Fourth Dance

In this dance, simply stand in one spot (preferably in the center of a magical runic circle) and spin while evoking the negative state of mind. You should do this exercise three times in a row and then rest. If a concentrated thought vacuum is attained, the effects of dizziness will be minimized. In any event, the student will want to rest with his or her head to the north at the conclusion of the exercise.

Fifth Dance

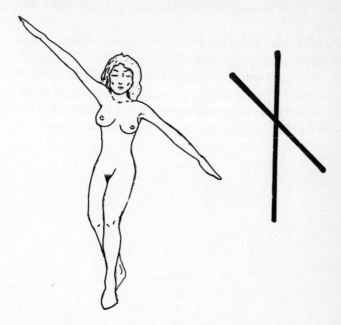

Facing north, take up the N-rune posture, perform a few preliminary breathing exercises, and then begin to sing or hum the *nnnnn* sound. Then put the right foot spread out sideways to the right, and remain in this position for about seven seconds while singing the *nnnnn* sound. You will still be facing north at this point. Then turn around 180 degrees on the right foot so that you are facing south. Remain in this position again for about seven seconds, but sing the *eeeee* sound. Now make the 180-degree turn on your left foot so that you are again facing north, and sing the *nnnnn* sound for another seven seconds. Turn again on the left foot to the south and sing the *eeeee* sound, and finally return to the north by pivoting on the right foot and conclude with the *nnnnn* sound. This whole cycle of movements is to be repeated at least three times. This exercise is actually a dynamic combination of the N- and E-runes into the HAGAL.

Another way to intensify the experience of some runic dance and postures is to use illumination from behind so that the postures throw shadows onto a wall. This form of "shadow dance" is especially powerful as a mode of evoking memories from ages past and as an enhancement of the runester's ability to read the runes in divinatory work.

Chapter 11

Runic Mudras

We have certain indications that manual signs of some kind must have been known in the ancient Germanic magical traditions. These indications include the use of the widely splayed hand and the "fig sign" (holding the thumb between the clenched index and middle fingers) as signs to ward off evil influences. But it was left to the German rune magicians to redevelop a full set of systematic magical hand gestures or postures (analogous to the mudras used in Indian yoga) for the runic tradition. This idea was first put forward by S. A. Kummer in his little book *Runen-Magie* (1933–34), and was furthered by Karl Spiesberger in his *Runenmagie* (1955).

Besides the rather sparse folkloristic indications of the traditional use of hand signs for magical purposes, there are strong hints in Old Norse literature of both the magical importance of the *hands* in general and the idea that magical powers can be sent from or contained in them. The most ancient and striking of these references are found in the "Sigrdrífumál" (stanzas 3, 8, and 10) in the *Poetic Edda*, where we read about the "healing hands" (more literally the hands of a physician) and about how runes are to be scratched on the backs of the hands, on the fingernails, and

113

on the palms. These are naturally only the very tip of a great iceberg of lore lying below the surface of what has survived of the ancient magical runic technology.

In general it can be said that the runic hand postures can be used in exactly the same kinds of ways that the body postures, or asanas, are used. Their advantage, of course, is that they can be more easily and discreetly performed. Therefore regular practice and actual use in critical magical situations is easier and more convenient. Any ritual or working that can be carried out with asanas can be done with the mudras as well. Whereas the full body postures make use of the various centers throughout the body, the hand signs must be more fully charged with the magical imagination of the runester, as he or she is only working with the two centers in the hands. The hands can, however, be brought into proximity with the other centers of the body to help increase the effectiveness of the mudra. To increase the intensity of the hand-signs with energy from bodily centers, the runester can use the Indian system of chakras, the Neo-Platonic system that survives in the Kabbalistic tradition, or the old Germanic system.

In the practice of healing, which is more fully discussed in chapter 13, the runic mudra to be used in healing a certain part of the body can be brought into direct contact with that region, or that region can be placed between two hands performing the corresponding magical hand sign.

As some of the oldest traditional references mentioned above would indicate, the runes can be used in magical conjunction with the hand centers without the specific use of runic hand signs. The runester can draw or paint a specific rune on the palm, nails, or back of the hand and strongly visualize the rune in a sphere of energy glowing around the hand. This can then be used to infuse an object with that particular runic force. There is also an important indication in traditional literature of the use of such practices in the charging of talismanic objects. The mudras, like the asanas, act as aids to concentration in the generation of rune might. After sufficient practice has been gained, it will soon be found that this force can be generated through a variety of means.

Practice of Runic Mudras

Before beginning the practice of any runic hand signs, prepare yourself with a few deep breaths in the I-rune posture. Engage the general streams of runic forces from above and below through the agency of the I-rune force. If possible, the runic hand sign should be made at eye level, directly in front of the face, at a distance of about one foot away from the head. This places the hand-center in a triangle with the pineal gland and the throat center, allowing the runic center to be charged with the might of the magical voice and breath, and to be perceived with the magical eye as well as with the physical ones.

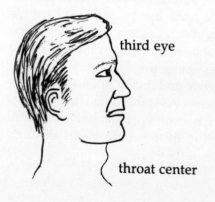

third eye

throat center

rune

While the rune sign is being produced, sing the appropriate runic mantras or songs while strongly visualizing the runic shape along the lines of the hand imitating the runic form.

It is suggested that the runester use the runic hand signs to run through the twelve runes indicated in Kummer's runic curriculum outlined in chapter 7. Otherwise any of the exercises you learn can be experimented with by making use of rune signs rather than postures or even carvings.

The Eighteen Runic Mudras of the Armanic Futhork

In performing these runic hand signs the runester should let experimentation be his or her guide. Try the gestures as shown, but also experiment with using the reverse polarity of some of the runes by using the hand opposite from the one shown. Each runic hand sign must be practiced until some sense of actual engagement with the corresponding runic force is perceived. You should aim for being able to practice the runic hand sign for at least ten minutes at a high level of concentration. This is best done through a regimen of practicing for three minutes, resting for a short time, then repeating the exercise for another three minutes, resting again, and finally intensely practicing for another three minutes. After this initial time of practice it will be found that it becomes progressively easier to call upon the manifestation of the runic forces through these or any other means.

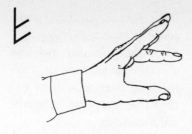

FA Sound formula: *ffffffff, fa-fe-fi-fo-fu*
Thoughts are to be focused on the generation of pure fire-produced power and love for the *Fa-tor* ("father") of all the worlds.

UR Sound formula: *uuuuu-uuu, uuuuurrrrr*
Thoughts are to be focused on the assimilation of primal power and knowledge, and on increasing magnetic forces.

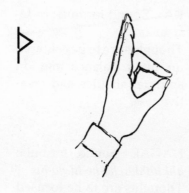

THORN Sound formula: *thththth, ta-the-thi-tho-thu* (Kummer also suggests *da-de-di-do-du*)
Thoughts are to be focused on receiving solar energy, circulating it throughout the whole body, and putting it at the disposal of the magical will.

OS Sound formula: *oooo-ooooo, ooooozzzzz*
Thoughts should not be directed or focused on anything in particular here except the reception of spiritual blessings.

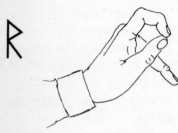

RIT Sound formula: *rrrrrrrr, ra-re-ri-ro-ru*
Thoughts are to be focused on the reception of higher counsel, on an innate sense of rightness, and on a perception of cosmic rhythm.

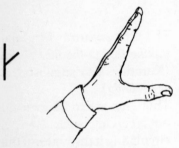

KA Sound formula: *ka-ke-ki-ko-ku*
Thoughts are to be centered on inner balance and on spiritual abilities and creativeness.

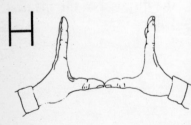

HAGAL Sound formula: *hhhhhhhh, ha-he-hi-ho-hu*
Thoughts are to be focused on universal love, on the will to highest attainment, and on the interconnectedness of the cosmos.

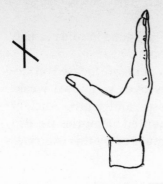

NOT   Sound formula: *nn-nnnnnn, na-ne-ni-no-nu*
Thoughts are to be concentrated on learning what one needs for development.

IS   Sound formula: *iiiiiiii, iiiiizzzzz*
Thoughts are to be focused on concentrating magical forces for the development of the self and on drawing these forces to yourself and holding them there.

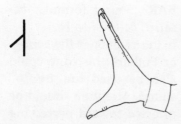

AR   Sound formula: *aaa-aaaaa,aaaaarrrrr*
Thoughts are to be directed toward the influx of the rejuvenating, renewing aspects of the solar power.

SIG Sound formula: *sssiiiig, sa-se-si-so-su*

Thoughts are focused on victory over your own weaknesses and faults. Ancient inherited memories are also stimulated by this exercise.

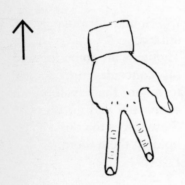

TYR Sound formula: *tyy-yrrrr, ta-te-ti-to-tu*

In the tradition of the Younger Futhark this rune could also be used for the "d" sound. Attention should be directed to learning of former lives, of previous manifestations of your self.

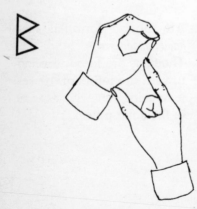

BAR Sound formula: *ba-aarrrr, ba-be-bi-bo-bu*

In the tradition of the Younger Futhark this rune could also be used for the "p" sound. Attention should be directed toward perceiving a birth, or a coming into being, of the personal spirit.

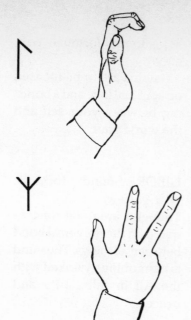

LAF Sound formula: *llllllll, llllllaaaaffff, la-le-li-lo-lu*
Thoughts are to be focused on gaining enlightenment of the self.

MAN Sound formula: *mm-mmmmmm, mmmmmaaaaaann, ma-me-mi-mo-mu*
This sign can ward off every danger. In the exercise, you should concentrate on the influx and outflow of electromagnetic rune might, which begins to awaken the power of divine magic.

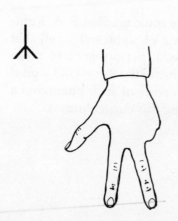

YR Sound formula: *yyy-yyrrrrrr*
This rune was generally avoided by Kummer in his explanations, as he considered it to be "demonic," which meant he often had erotic ideas in mind. The work of Karl Spiesberger fills in this gap—he suggests that the mudra be used to liberate the magician from instinctive compulsions through conscious control of the self.

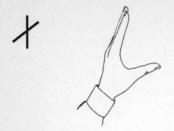

EH   Sound formula: *eeee-eeeeeee*
Thoughts are to be focused on spiritual love and a bonding between your self and the world soul.

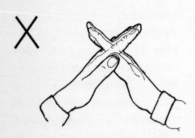

GIBOR   Sound   formula: *ga-ge-gi-go-gu*
Thoughts are to be concentrated on the universal bond between all things. The mind is harmoniously linked with the All in full clarity and peace.

In his descriptions of these runic mudras, S. A. Kummer often refers to phenomena of sight and smell that should accompany the successful performance of these hand signs. The research branches of the Rune-Gild would be interested in hearing any reports of such phenomena from those who are undertaking this curriculum.

Chapter 12

Steads of Rune Might

S ome references have already been made in other chapters to the preferability of certain directional orientations when performing runic postures, and to the importance of the runester's relationship to the land under his or her feet when performing runic exercises. There is really a whole science, or body of lore, that has to do with "earth magic," or geomancy, which corresponds to the German forms of rune magic. This was more or less taken into account by all the German rune magicians, but F. B. Marby seems to have developed this branch of knowledge to its highest level.

In theory we must take several factors into consideration: (1) the orientation of the runester (what direction he or she will be facing), (2) the timing of the exercise, and (3) the actual place, or "stead," in which the work will take place. This last element is further divided into two categories: (a) the point on the earth's surface where the work is to take place, and (b) the spatial environment in which the runester will do the exercise.

There are some generally beneficial conditions that, if care is taken to ensure them, will greatly enhance the power and efficacy of any runic exercise. There are also other special environmental circumstances that are arranged for specific magical effects. To ensure maximal power, the runester should give some attention to some or all factors discussed in this chapter.

First there is the question of the laying out of a magical circle. This may or may not normally be a part of a runester's way of working. Some magicians like to set a definite boundary to the area in which they work, and some feel that such circles are necessary to keep out negative or distracting influences. This aspect of the work is discretionary, depending on one's normal practice. A circle does aid in the regular performance of rune magic of this kind when it is necessary to determine exact points of the compass and other factors relating to the orientation of the runester on the surface of the earth and its electromagnetic sphere.

To construct a useful magical circle in the open air, you will need wooden pins or small stakes, some thread or twine, and a compass. Determine where you want the center of your circle to be and put a stake there. Set the compass on or right beside it. Determine magnetic north. Using the thread or twine to align it, put another stake seven to nine feet away from your center in the direction of magnetic north. The compass will also show you where true north is. Place another stake there, and using that as a point of orientation, determine the other three cardinal points of direction. Place stakes in these four compass points as well. The more traditional folk will also want to place similar stakes and lines in the "cross quarter" points, halfway between each of the four cardinal points, so that the circle is divided into eight equal parts. However, the division of the circle into four parts is quite adequate for most purposes. If possible, it is good to have the runes drawn around the rim of the circle, so that for the Armanen tradition the runic circle might appear something like the one seen in Figure 12.1.

Figure 12.1   A Runic Magical Circle

In general it is suggested that the runester always orient him/herself toward the north while doing rune exercises. This maximizes the harmonious flow of electromagnetic (or od-magnetic) streams and currents according to most rune magicians. Other directions are used only in specific types of operations or by those whose aims correspond to the kinds of modulations of the electromagnetic streams flowing through those lines. There is another powerful flow of force that is generally found to stream from the east to the west, or from the right to the left if one is facing north. This is why the flow of runic force is directed into the right side and out the left in many of the runic exercises in chapter 7. When facing east there is a flow of electromagnetic force from the north to the south, or from the left to right. The science of the magical use of the electromagnetic streams in the environment is very well developed in the Tantric traditions of India, and it would be very helpful for most runesters to become familiar with this system.

Timing

Before delving further into the lore of using the spatial environment for rune-magic ends, it is necessary to talk about the "place in time" in which the exercises are to occur. In theory there are at least two factors taken into consideration here: (1) the time of the year (or phase of moon, etc.), and (2) the time of day.

When considering the time of day, both symbolic and natural factors should be taken into account. In symbolism (which for some may supersede any natural factors) the dawn is used for new beginnings, the noontide for the victory of consciousness, twilight for transformational, or change-causing work, and the midnight hour is for deep delvings into the unconscious and the unknown. F. B. Marby suggests using all four of these times, but to avoid facing south in the summer. The main natural factor to be considered, which Marby emphasizes, is the avoidance of high levels of ultraviolet rays. These are very disturbing and even destructive to the harmonious and healthy flow of runic streams in the terrestrial zones (zones 3 and 4). In fact, any time is fine for runic exercise. These suggestions are meant merely to indicate when the natural or symbolic forces are most likely to be beneficial.

Astrology can be brought into the timing of runic exercises as well. By keying runic exercises to the lunar cycle, the runester can work with expanding (electric) runes during the waxing and full moon (especially with the MAN-rune at the tide of the full moon) and with contracting (magnetic) runes during the waning and new moon. Correspondences between planetary and/or zodiacal forces and the runes have been suggested by many of the Armanic rune magicians. But since the astrological system inherited from the Middle East is not really a part of the Teutonic runic tradition, there is no agreement on how these correspondences are to be made. We still await the full redevelopment of a Teutonic astrology, for which pioneering work has been done by Robert Zoller of the Rune-Gild.

One logical and reliable use of runes for timing of work throughout the year is provided by linking the 16 Old Norse *mál* ("times") to the 16 runes of the Younger Futhark. This was done by Roland Dionys Jossé in his *Die Tala der Raunen* (1955), from which Table 12.1 has been adapted. In this table it can be seen when the mál ruling each of the 16 runes begins, and when the time of day similarly ruled by that rune begins. Jossé suggests that the day times be keyed to central European time (i.e., one hour earlier than Greenwich mean time), but that is optional.

Table 12.1 The Runic *Mál*-Tides for the Year and Day

Rune	The Year-*Mál*	Beginning of Day-*Mál*
Fe	22 December–12 January	12:00 Midnight
Ur	13 January–3 February	1:30 A.M.
Thurs	4 February–25 February	3:00 A.M.
Oss	26 February–20 March	4:30 A.M.
Reidh	21 March–12 April	6:00 A.M.
Kaun	13 April–5 May	7:30 A.M.
Hagall	6 May–28 May	9:00 A.M.
Naudh	29 May–20 June	10:30 A.M.
Iss	21 June–14 July	12:00 Noon
Ar	15 July–7 August	1:30 P.M.
Sol	8 August–30 August	3:00 P.M.
Tyr	31 August–22 September	4:30 P.M.
Bjarkan	23 September–15 October	6:00 P.M.
Logr	16 October–7 November	7:30 P.M.
Madhr	8 November–29 November	9:00 P.M.
Yr	30 November–21 December	10:30 P.M.

Rune Steads

The two factors to be taken into account here are intriguing topics. The first involves the actual determination of given places (points on the surface of the land) that are likely to be steads where great amounts of electromagnetic, odic force converge and/or accumulate. It is not really necessary to believe in the objective reality of such things, or to believe in their efficiency in enhancing magical endeavors, to symbolically make use of some of the lore of "power points." Magicians sensitive to certain terrains or spatial environments know how a hill, a rock, or other natural or artificial features can be evocative of certain powerful moods, or be suggestive of things that lie beyond normal perception. To some extent the lore of the steads of rune might take advantage of this. The European practitioner has many advantages in that he or she can often find and practice in ancient sites where some related magic, if not rune magic itself, was worked on a regular basis in ages past. If such steads can be found, they should be used if possible.

However, the forces underlying the original choice of a given stead for magical activity are at work everywhere, not only in those places that were used for such work in ancient times. Power points can be found and used wherever you are in the world. There are many ways of finding such steads of might. Perhaps the most useful is the direct application of intuition. Simply walk or hike in an area where you want to hunt such power points. Remain attentive to your purpose of finding such a stead, but be relaxed and patient in your search. When you find places that seem to your eye to be likely candidates for such steads, perform the I-rune exercise on the spot and record your results. (Of course, those places that fit one of the five spatial configurations outlined below would be prime candidates for consideration.) If you feel a marked increase in rune might in a certain location, you are likely to have found a stead of might. Keep looking everywhere you go, and when you find a stead, mark it in some secret way so that you can return to it. In North America many such power points were identified by native American shamans, but in large measure modern individual runesters are in the same situation as the ancient runesters in Europe were—they must seek out these steads for themselves.

Other methods may also be applied in the hunting of these steads. Practices such as dowsing, star-sighting, or ideas akin to those used in Chinese *feng shui* are very useful in identifying steads of rune might.

The second factor to be considered regarding the use of space in rune magic is the choice of spatial environment in which to practice the exercises. Many runesters will, of course, have to content themselves most often with practicing indoors. But it will be noticed that if you experiment with doing the exercises outdoors on the bare ground, the efficiency and power of the work will be greatly enhanced. There are five types of spatial environments for runic experimentation that are identified by Marby. Each has its special function, but as always, let your own experience be your most reliable guide. These environments were first described by Marby in his *Marby-Runen-Bücherei* (vol. 5/6, pp. 74–112) and later in his *Der Weg zu den Müttern* (1957). In theory the runester will be radiating a certain force during the exercises that, if given free room, will form a sphere around the physical body. The physical environment modulates and redirects this force in certain predictable ways, much as the body of a musical instrument modulates the sounds produced by its strings. This sphere of force can be modulated in five ways:

1. 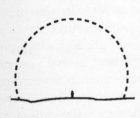 The runester stands on a level surface and the sphere of power is divided—half in zone 3, wave space, and half reaching down into zone 4, earth space. It might actually be best if the runester stands on a slight elevation of about three feet. The overall effect of this environment is balance between all realms—between the earthly streams and the cosmic ones. This is especially useful for operations emphasizing sober, balanced, everyday pursuits.

2.

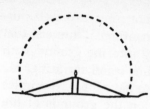

If the runester stands on an artificial tower or platform the field of activity in the wave space will be increased. There will be added influx from that zone, and the effects of the exercise will be more direct in that zone. In ancient Germanic magical practice it was often reported that magicians would perform magic from atop a platform called a *seidh-stallr*. Note that this arrangement largely separates, or insulates, the runester from the material earthspace. Even from below, great amounts of energy present in the wave space are made available. This effect can also be partially achieved when exercises are done on any artificial flooring. Those positions in which the runester is separated from the earth streams, or where exposure to the atmospheric streams is maximized, lead to an influx of new ideas and access to visions of the future.

3.

Another way of gaining an effect similar to the one obtained with the platform is to do the exercises from high atop a natural peak or steep hill. The difference is that the runester is still in contact with the material earth-current, which is often intensified at this point as it spirals up to a point through the conical structure of the raised earth. In this way, the impulses available from the free wave space are maximized and coupled with the intense focus of material earth-streams. This combination is especially potent in work intended to convert spiritual visions or impulses into material reality.

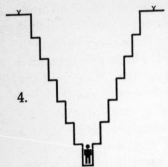

4.

Marby dedicated a large part of his book *Der Weg zu den Müttern* to the topic of runic exercises performed in artificial "funnels" that were dug into the ground with descending spiral terracing. He claimed to have found examples of these on the grounds of the Gertrudenberg near Osnabruck. (It is worth pointing out that the very name of the city Osnabruck means "bridge of the gods.") By performing runic exercises in such a place, the runester can increase the influx of earth streams and minimize the volume of atmospheric streams. Another way of gaining a similar effect is, of course, to do runic exercises in a natural valley or deep depression in the earth. As with the exercise on the conical uplift in number three above, the intense focus of atmospheric force may be increased as it spirals down into the depression. In this configuration the influx of new ideas is held to a minimum, while access to old experiences is sharpened and clarified, and old ideas are ripened and evolved. This is an ideal configuration for work on developing that which you already are—refining and making conscious the contents of the memory.

5.

In this configuration the runester is totally enclosed within a subterranean space—a cave, artificial cell, passageway, or underground hall. Such structures are quite common in various parts of central and northern Europe, many of which date from the Bronze Age. Guido von List describes in detail this kind of structure, which is found in his native Lower Austria, throughout his study *Deutsch-mythologische Landschaftsbilder.* In this environment the inflow of earth streams is maximized and raised to its highest intensity. These streams and the ancient (transpersonal) memories that they have stored up are channeled into the consciousness of the runester and made available in great quantities.

Chapter 13

Healing Runes

The runes have been used since the most ancient times for magical healing, as well as for harming. Some of the lore presented in chapter 11 on runic hand signs will be further developed here, as the "healing hands" spoken of by the valkyrie Sigrdrífa are something that the runic practitioner will want to have at his or her command.

The use of runes for purposes of healing physical and psychological disorders was taught by both F. B. Marby and S. A. Kummer. It was, however, Kummer who taught them in a way that became useful to later German rune magicians such as K. Spiesberger. It is mainly the lore taken from the methods taught by Kummer and Spiesberger that I draw on here to outline a working system of runic healing.

Runes are used essentially for two kinds of healing. The first kind is a general, nonspecific, therapeutic application of rune might to ensure good health and physical strength and endurance. The other kind is the application of rune might to specific health complaints. Marby and Kummer were always fond of pointing out how their students, when regularly performing a curriculum of runic exercises, would begin to enjoy better health, and that whatever chronic complaints they might have had would seem to be alleviated.

The theories as to how runic healing works vary. But a common thread running throughout them all is the idea that the runes (the mysteries themselves) are closely linked to the body through the conscious exercise of runic yoga and mantra. The runes are thought to represent a hidden universal system that vibrates according to correct harmonies. When the exercises are engaged in, the body begins to resonate with this universal runic harmony, and thus good health results. The runic shapes and sounds work from the atomic level, up through the molecular level and into the cellular level, where the health of the individual is directly affected. The alignment of the body in the physical shape of the runes can be seen as analogous to the correct and harmonious alignment of atoms in a crystal, and the right tones activate this alignment so that the natural harmonies are balanced and intensified.

This same general theory is also good for parts of the psychosomatic complex that have become diseased, which have fallen out of harmony with the right runic order. More pointed and focused amounts of specific sorts of rune might must be directed to those regions of the body affected so as to re-harmonize them. It is, however, most often found that for the rune magician, the power of the runes will greatly enhance his or her overall health, and that most diseases can be staved off by using general or specific rune exercises. (It has been some eight or nine years since the author of this book has had a common cold.)

In practice the runester will perhaps want to heal others of various complaints. (Of course, the use of runes for healing purposes should always be used in conjunction with other treatments.) The practice of runic healing is quite simple. The "patient" should lie down on a bed or sofa with his or her head to the north. The runic healer will stand behind (to the north of) the patient, thus standing in the path of the normal north-south flow of terrestrial electromagnetic current. The runester can then act as a sort of "filter" of naturally occurring forces, remodulating them toward the improved health of the patient.

With all workings of runic healing the healer will spend a good deal of time engaging in a sphere or current common to both the patient and him/herself. This is done with the repeated chanting of the vocalic runes *A-E-I-O-U*. (This is the order used by the Armanic magicians; other orders can be used by those who know them.) The point of this is to engage in a stream or sphere of force with the patient in order to enter into an empathetic state with him or her. It is important for the runic healer to realize at this point, and to repeatedly realize it every time he or she enters into such an operation, that the disorders of the patient will have no effect on the health of the healer.

Once this state of empathy has been achieved, the runic healer can use the I-rune to reharmonize the general health of the patient. The rune posture should be struck and the runic sound sung as in the normal practice of the runester. It is always an option to just sing the mantra and visualize the rune might flowing to the patient, or this can be done along with the performance of the runic asana. First, face in the direction most suited to drawing the runic force to you, and then face south, toward the patient, and let the force flow out to him or her. This practice can be followed with all the runic exercises in this chapter.

If the patient does not know what the problem actually is but suspects a specific ailment, the runic healer can engage in a diagnostic exercise using the H-rune mudra. Both hands are passed over the body of the reclining patient, and an attempt is made to sense where the problem lies. Experience is essential here.

At the conclusion of the operation, reverse the order of

vowels: *U-O-I-E-A*, and withdraw from the empathetic state with the patient. Again, remember that no ill effects will result.

If the patient comes with a specific problem, or you have determined what it might be, then specific runes can be used to treat that disorder. The practice is exactly as was outlined for general purposes with the I-rune. Sing the appropriate mantras in a low voice (but one definitely audible to the patient) and assume the rune posture; and at least for the most experienced, strongly visualize the colors of the healing runes flowing into the affected region. Kummer suggests that the colors will more or less come on their own and should not be forced by the practitioner.

Besides the use of the body postures while standing to the north of the patient, the experienced healer can also apply the runic hand sign directly to the afflicted part of the body. The hands are charged with the rune might by means of the runic mudra, or the runes are painted or drawn on the hands as suggested in chapter 12. First the mudra is used to pass close to the affected region, and then to actually touch it.

It should be noted that Kummer suggests that the healer use certain combinations of runes for specific regions of the body or kinds of ailments. If two runes are involved, *both* are to be used equally and visualized together in a common sphere of rune might.

For head complaints and fevers: FA (shining red).
For neck, liver, or nerve complaints: IS (bright blue) and UR (orange).
For depression, glandular inflammation, or swelling of the lymph nodes: EH (bright yellow).
For problems in the chest or lungs: OTHIL (bright violet) and UR (orange).

For ailments of the chest, back, or heart: OTHIL (bright violet) and the cross posture (pink).

For problems in the digestive organs: IS (bright blue) and KA (white with a yellow tinge).

For kidney or bladder problems, or pain in the lumbar region: HAGAL (bright green) and the cross posture (pink).

For infections or skin diseases: NOT (dark red) and LAF (fire red).

For bleeding external injuries: IS (bright blue) and MAN (purple-red).

For injuries to the bones or skin: FA (bright red).

For nervous complaints or pain in the tendons: SIG (pure blue) and MAN (purple-red).

For diseases of the blood, gout, rheumatism, or hardening of the arteries: IS (bright blue) and TYR (pure gray).

These are the essential points in the practice of runic healing. This art is the special field of true healers, and those with talent already developed in this area are encouraged to develop the practice of runic healing beyond these basic levels.

Chapter 14

The Working of
the Graal-Cup

The magical theme of the Graal, or Grail, is very strong in the German rune-magic traditions of the early part of this century. Those traditions took their magical lore concerning the Graal from Wagner's modern mythos, from the medieval traditions of the epic *Parzival* by Wolfram von Eschenbach, as well as from the magical lore surrounding the Graal developed by Lanz von Liebenfels and other occultists.

For the working presented here, we are again indebted to S. A. Kummer, who outlined it in his short work *Runen-Magie.* For Kummer the MAN-rune is a powerful tool for interacting with the upper zones, or with the divine realms. In this working the MAN-rune exercise is expanded into a new quality of experience in which the runester is flooded with waves from the upper zones and gains direct communication with the Graal itself.

To begin with, perform the MAN-rune exercise for at least 20 minutes in preparation (see chapter 7). Remember, to begin this exercise you must spend some time in the I-rune posture doing some deep breathing exercises. Then lift the arms to form the MAN-rune posture, with the arms out at a 45-degree angle. The palms are face up and slightly cupped. Next sing or hum the *mmmmmmm* sound, letting the tone rise and fall in a siren-like fashion. If your arms become tired, let them rest for a while in the I-rune posture, but keep the *mmmmmmmm* sound in force. During this phase concentrate fully on the direct reception of currents of energy from the upper zones, which enter through the back of your head and through both palms. These three streams converge in the center of the chest, in the region of the thymus gland, where they stimulate the spleen and the sympathetic nerve and circulate about the solar plexus. From there they will at first flow out through the legs into the ground. Some of the energy will, however, also stream from the region of the solar plexus directly into the aura (or personal energy field surrounding the runester) through the navel.

This exercise should be repeated until you can comfortably do it for 30 minutes. At the conclusion of the MAN-rune exercise, always take a few deep breaths while visualizing the excess accumulated force being drained off, or grounded, into the earth. You may find it helpful to shift all your weight onto your right foot while doing this.

Again, the Working of the Graal-Cup is only to be undertaken after you have been doing the MAN-rune exercise for at least 20 minutes. This is to ensure that your energy system is sufficiently loaded with od-magnetic force and that the flow of force through the head and arms is strong enough.

After the MAN-waves are flowing, take up the M-rune posture again, as shown in Figure 14.1, with the head tilted back, eyes gazing upward into the All, and the right foot only lightly resting on the ground. The effect of this is to block significant outflow of the streaming force into the ground so that it accumulates, thus intensifying the levels of energy available to the centers in the middle of the body. A network of energy very similar to a cup or funnel shape will develop around your body while doing this exercise. To some extent this will also be found in doing the regular form of the MAN-rune.

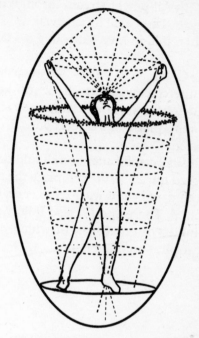

Figure 14.1   Manifestation of the Graal-Cup

Sing the *mmmmmm* sound while activating this network and increasing the outflow of backed-up energies through the navel. You can expect to have some prickling sensations around the navel during this phase of the working, as the cup or chalice effect becomes stronger and stronger.

Now begin to sing *oooooommmmmm*, while visualizing rings of force emanating from the mouth and enveloping the entire body. As the feeling of the chalice effect becomes very strong, you can invoke the particular powers or qualities toward which you are questing. Kummer used the following:

> Fa-tor, I call to Thee,
> With All-power stream through me,
> The Graal in me awake,
> Threefold in love oaths to Tyr I take!

Next the Graal can be intensified even further by turning in a counterclockwise direction, still keeping all the weight on the left foot, while rhythmically singing the formulas. It is in this phase that direct counsel, or knowledge, can be expected.

In conclusion, careful attention should be paid to draining the gathered forces. To do this, place the right foot firmly on the ground and allow the excess energies to flow out into the ground. There should also follow a period of at least ten minutes of quiet rest, in which time flashes of insight and inspiration often come.

Chapter 15

The Ritual of
the Ninth Night

In his *Die "Edda" als Schlüssel des kommenden Weltalters!* (The *Edda* as Key to the Coming Age) the theosophist and mantra expert Peryt Shou presented a highly complex working essentially based on the concept of the NOT-rune, coupled with the mythic formula of "Odin's Cry of Need." In the *Edda* ("Hávamál" stanzas 138–139) there is a description of Odin's runic initiation in which he is said to hang for nine nights on the World Tree, wounded by his spear, until on the ninth night he discovers and "takes up" the runes. The phrase *æpandi nam* is found in the Old Norse original, and this literally means "[I] took [the runes] screaming." Here this is turned into a mantric formula by Shou as the key to this working.

Shou's presentation and point of view is significantly different from that of List, Marby, Kummer, or Spiesberger. The function of this exercise is something akin to that of the Graal-Cup in chapter 14, but it is far more complex. Shou sees this exercise as a mode of communication between an elect on this planet and an extraterrestrial "League of Truth." He considers the Coming Age to be one in which the obsolete form of the Christian God of death will be superseded by a living, resurrected form in the body of the elect themselves. Shou identifies this God as Wuotan-Hermes, or Wuotan-Christ. The collective body of the elect will transform their bodies into new, higher forms, and will thereby be said to have "stepped down from the cross." This is to be facilitated through spiritual exercises such as the Ninth Night. As Shou himself puts it: "The descent of Odin from the World Tree is the secret of the 'od-ization' of the ego ('I')." This constitutes the resurrection within the elect.

Shou understands this exercise as a way to transform the body of the magician into an "antenna" for certain cosmic streams of power. In this he is on the same wavelength, so to speak, as the other rune magicians of his time. That this book first appeared in 1920 might also suggest that Shou was among the first to conceive of runic exercises in this way. The author explains this process in the following way:

> The material substance of the ego is transformed into a more refined "odic" one through the power of this ritual. It is the material of the body which is the same, but it assumes another vibratory form, one in which it becomes obedient and subordinated to the Logos, while the natural material body is antagonistic to the Logos. The latter is bound to the instincts by sin. Thus only by means of "need" does the transformation, the awakening to Od-in occur. The sinful flesh does not voluntarily dissolve itself into the vibratory form of the spiritual-divine, of odic corporality.

Here it is clear that Shou has a basically Gnostic outlook on this particular work. He also was constantly trying to reconcile Roman Catholicism with the Germanic tradition. Regardless of what one might think of his theories, the basic mode of his working is one very much worth examining and experiencing.

That collective entity with which the antenna effects

communication is called Mercury-Wuotan, and it is said not to be a single being but rather an interplanetary network of radio waves between the planet Mercury and the Earth, constituting the League of Truth, or the "Brotherhood of Hermes-Wuotan." The celestial antenna that corresponds to the one set up by the runester, which is supposed to act as a kind of transmitter for the League of Truth, is said by Shou to be situated in the constellation of the Swan (Cygnus), which according to Shou has nine stars arranged in the following pattern:

This may not be astronomically correct, but it is how Shou schematically depicts it. Now, before any reader starts to get too smug about dismissing these ideas about "transmitters," and "antennas," it might be well to note that Shou was writing around 1920—some 20 years before radio astronomy was first used. By the mid-1940s, a point in the Cygnus constellation had in fact been identified as a galaxy

(Cygnus A) that emitted large amounts of radio waves!*
According to Shou: "Everything that we discover in nature
is an external projection of the interior man according to the
law of psycho-physical parallelism. Everything—including the radio-telegraph—is within us. And so we create it in
the exterior world!"

The Practice of the
Ritual of the Ninth Night

The actual working of this rite involves practicing a
series of exercises over the course of several days or even
weeks, depending on the subjective perceptions of the
individual. The whole rite is divided into two main phases
or operations.

First Operation

In this operation the runester activates the outer vibratory ring (square *CDEF*)† supported by the central
staff (*ABF*).

1. Stand facing the north (toward the constellation Cygnus
if possible) in the I-rune posture and concentrate on the
feet while singing the mantra *æp* (pronounced as the *ap* in
apt). The force is slowly drawn up through the feet to a point
(*B*) in the center of the chest (in the thymus region). Repeat
this exercise until successful. (Note: If you have been working other runic exercises, the technical aspects of the Ritual
of the Ninth Night will, of course, proceed at a more rapid
pace.)

---

*Information on this radio emission by Cygnus A is available in any basic
astronomy textbook—for example, Isaac Asimov, *The Universe* (New York: Dis-
cus, 1968), pp. 284 ff.

†For the sake of convenience and clarity, all references to the geometrical
points of the antenna structure to be activated refer to Figure 15.1, while references to the mantric formula are depicted in Figure 15.2

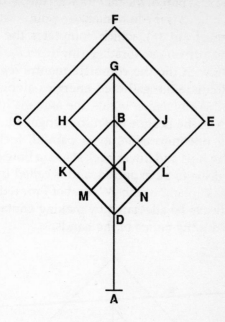

Figure 15.1   The Geometrical Outline of the
Antenna Structure for the Ritual of the Ninth Night

2. Now stretch your arms straight out in the cross posture
and sing the mantric syllable *and* (pronounced "ah-nd"). At
this time visualize a beam of force (*ABE*) with terminals in
the middle of both palms. You may notice that there will be
a slight prickling sensation in the hand centers during this
phase. The correct performance of this mantric phase involves maximizing the nasal quality of the *annnn* sound.
This is done by progressively pressing the back of the
tongue into the soft palate, or the back of the roof of the
mouth. Be very conscious of the transition from the *an* to
the *d* sound. Repeat this exercise until you are satisfied that
success has been attained.

3. Finish the first part of the mantra with the *i* ("ee") sound. When the *i* sound is made, visualize a point just above the crown of the head (F), which completes the full cross-antenna and the outer vibratory ring (CDEF). Repeat the whole cycle with the the complete mantra *æp-and-i*, and begin to circulate the gathered energies along the *ADEF* course. As this circulation builds, the antenna to the spiritual network of the League of Truth is engaged. There may develop an uncomfortable, even painful, feeling in the region of the hips and lower back at some time during this exercise. This is to be expected, and is called by Shou the "Wound of Wuotan," or the "Wound of Prometheus." This pain can always be alleviated by making contact with the hipbones with the palms of the hands.

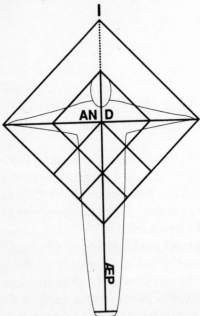

Figure 15.2   The Antenna Structures and Mantric Formulas for the Ritual of the Ninth Night

4. At some point in this phase the inner vibratory ring (*GHIJ*) will be opened, or better said, it will open itself. This will signal that the *And-vari*, or dwarf of the subatomic force of matter, has been overcome and released into the inner Ring-Pass-Not.

5. At this point the whole *æpandi nam* mantra is to be brought into action. This is done by repeating the exercise as outlined in phases 1–4 above: (a) sing the *æp* with the arms outstretched, (b) place the palms on the hipbones during the *andi* phase, and then (c) repeat the whole *æpandi* mantra with the arms again in the cross posture. Now sing the syllable *nam* ("nah-m") and again touch the hipbones with your palms. This creates a third vibratory ring (*BKDL*). Shou actually recommends that you hold off the *nam* phase as long as you can, until the growing pain in the hip region becomes so great that you *need* to alleviate it with the performance of the *nam* gesture. In this phase attention should be fully focused on the mid-chest point (*B*), with all other phenomena peripheral to that point. Shou further points out that the result of all this should be an intense feeling of energy and hyper-awareness. If a trance state or a feeling of psychological unease ensues, the exercise should be broken off. With the activation of the third vibratory ring, or "Golden Rectangle," full contact with the higher zone has been effected, and the runester can begin to expect direct communication in some form from the League of Truth, or the Brotherhood of Wuotan.

6. After success has been gained with phases 1–5 of the ritual, and a solid link between the runester and the network in the higher zones has been established, the practitioner undertakes a transformative, or rebirthing, phase in which he or she actually "gives birth" to a higher ego-form. This is done by first visualizing a concave, shieldlike form in front of but very close to the lower body, with its center at

the navel. On the inside of this surface, visualize an S-rune

in the form ∿ and sing the mantra *ansur* (a form of the name of the fourth rune: *ansuz* = Od-in). With repetition, there will begin to develop a body of light on the inside surface of this shield. This is a spiritual "placenta" for the reborn ego. It is fed by nine shining streams of magical "milk" emanating from the navel. This embryonic entity is protected by the shield as it grows with each repetition of the exercise.

Second Operation

The phases of establishing communication with the League of Truth and the generation of a higher ego stemming from the growth that has taken place in the psyche are now complete. It is now time to go on to more active stages.

7. Proceed as before, engaging all three vibratory rings as you have learned to do it with the mantric formula: *æpandi nam*, and *ansur* (if the last is still necessary). Now the spiritual eye (which is actually housed in the middle of the chest, in the thymus region) is "sacrificed," is given into "Mimir's Well."* The Well of Mimir is created by forming a fourth vibratory ring of power (*IMDN*) and circulating the power within it with the mantric formula *hva* (*hhhhh-vvvvvaaaaah*) while the runester is in the *nam*-posture. This is done by visualizing a point of light descending from the thymus region into the middle of the ring (*IMDN*). Now put your arms back into the cross posture and wait for an answering "echo" returning from the well in the form of inspiration, insight, and memories of things never before known.

---

*This is a reference to a myth concerning the Norse god Odin/Wuotan, who pledges one of his eyes to gain the knowledge and wisdom housed in the well of a giant named Mimir, whose name signifies memory.

8. Once success has been attained in this exercise, go on to the next mantric formula: *hvas (hhhhvvvvvaaaaaazzzzzzz)* in the cross posture. Feel the energy pulse from the middle of your body and reverberate back from the points of the outer vibratory ring (*CDEF*). In addition to this formula, the alternate *svar (zzzzzvvvvvaaaaah-rrrrrrrr)* can also be sung in this phase. In the final phase of the Ritual of the Ninth Night the runester has fully created the antenna-work within his or her body, and a highly articulate interchange is possible between the runester and that transpersonal network conceived of by Shou as the League of Truth.

Appendix

On Pronunciation

Those unfamiliar with the pronunciation of German or other continental languages will perhaps need some assistance in the correct performance of the basic sound values of the mantric formulas. This guide will enable everyone to perform most of the sounds flawlessly.

The Vowels

a   as in *father*
e   as in *gate*
i   as in *fleet*
o   as in *go*
u   as in *rule*

These vowel sounds are to be kept pure and simple at all times. When making each of them there should be no movement in the jaw.

The Consonants

f   as in modern English
th   as a simple *t*, or as the *th* in *thin*
r   trilled in the back of the throat (as in German or French) or in the front of the mouth (as in Spanish)
k   as in modern English

h   as in modern English at the front of a word, but silent following vowels
n   as in modern English
s   as *z* in *zero* when in initial position or between vowels, or as *ss* in *glass* in final position. Can also get the *z* sound in final position in some mantras, as shown in text.
t   as in modern English
b   as in modern English
l   as in modern English
m   as in modern English
g   always "hard," as the *g* in *go*

Pronunciation of the Armanic Rune Names

As a sample of how the above rules would be used, I present here popularized phonetic versions of the names of the 18 runes of the Armanic Futhork.

FA	[fah]
UR	[ooh-r]
THORN	[torn]
OS	[oh-ss]
RIT	[reet]
KA	[kah]
HAGAL	[hah-gal]
NOT	[noht, as in *note*]
IS	[ee-ss]
AR	[ah-r]
SIG	[zeeg]
TYR	[teer]
BAR	[bah-r]
LAF	[lah-f]
MAN	[mah-n]
YR	[ee-r]
EH	[ay, as in *lay*]
GIBOR	[gee-boh-r]

Bibliography

Books

Balzli, Johannes. *Guido von List: Der Wiederentdecker uralter arischer Weisheit.* Vienna: Guido-von-List-Gesellschaft, 1917.

Bienert, Josef. *Raunende Runen.* Winnenden: Rubin Verlag, 1964.

Blachetta, Walther. *Das Buch der deutschen Sinnzeichen.* Berlin-Lichterfelde: Widukind/Boss, 1941.

Brennen, J. H. *The Occult Reich.* New York: Signet, 1974.

Bülow, Werner von. *Der Ewigkeitsgehalt der eddischen Runen und Zahlen.* Munich: H. Stiegeler, 1925.

Flowers, Stephen E. *Runes and Magic: Magical Formulaic Elements in the Older Runic Tradition.* Berne: Lang, 1986.

Goodrick-Clarke, Nicholas. *The Occult Roots of Nazism.* Wellingborough, Northamptonshire: Aquarian, 1985.

Gorsleben, Rudolf John. *Die Hoch-Zeit der Menschheit.* Leipzig: Koehler & Amelang, 1930.

Heinz, Ulrich Jürgen. *Die Runen.* Freiburg/Breisgau: Bauer, 1987.

Hemberger, Adolf. *Organizationsformen, Rituale, Lehren, und magische Thematik der freimauerischen und freimauerartigen Bünde im deutschen Sprachraum Mitteleuropas. Teil I. Der mystisch-magische Orden Fraternitas Saturni.* Frankfurt/Main: Dr. A. Hemberger, [1971].

157

Hollander, Lee M. *The Poetic Edda*. 2d ed. Austin, TX: University of Texas Press, 1962.

Hunger, Ulrich. *Die Runenkunde im Dritten Reich*. Bern: Lang, 1984.

Jossé, Roland Dionys. *Die Tala der Raunen (Runo-astrologische Kabbalistik) Handbuch der Deutung des Wesens und Weges eines Menschen auf Grund der in seinem Namen verborgenen Sckicksalsraunen*. Freiburg: Bauer, 1955.

Kosbab, Werner. *Das Runen-Orakel*. Freiburg: Bauer, 1982.

Kummer, Siegfried Adolf. *Heilige Runenmacht*. Hamburg: Uranus-Verlag, 1932.

———. *Runen-Magie*. Dresden: Gartmann, 1933/34.

Kurtzahn, E. Tristan. *Die Runen als Heilszeichen und Schicksalslose*. Bad Oldesloe: Uranus, 1924.

List, Guido von. *Deutsch-mythologische Landschaftsbilder*. 2 vols. Berlin: H. Lustenoder, 1891.

———. *Das Geheimnis der Runen*. Vol. 1, *Guido-von-List-Bücherei*. Gross-Lichterfelde: P. Zillmann, 1908.

———. *Die Ursprache der Ario-Germanen und ihre Mysteriensprache*. Vol. 6, *Guido-von-List-Bücherei*. Vienna: Guido-von-List-Gesellschaft, 1914.

———. *The Secret of the Runes*. Translated by Stephen E. Flowers. Rochester, VT: Destiny, 1988.

Marby, Friedrich Bernhard. *Runenschrift, Runenwort, Runengymnastik* Vol. 1/2, *Marby-Runen-Bücherei*. Stuttgart: Marby Verlag, 1931.

———. *Marby-Runen-Gymnastik* Vol. 3/4, *Marby-Runen-Bücherei*. Stuttgart: Marby Verlag, 1932.

———. *Rassische Gymnastik als Aufrassungsweg*. Vol. 5/6, *Marby-Runen-Bücherei*. Stuttgart: Marby Verlag, 1935.

———. *Die Rosengarten und das ewige Land der Rasse*. Vol. 7/8, *Marby-Runen-Bücherei*. Stuttgart: Marby Verlag, 1935.

———. *Die Drei Schwäne*. Stuttgart: Marby Verlag, 1957.

———. *Der Weg zu den Müttern*. Stuttgart: Spieth Verlag, 1977. [orig. 1957]

Müller, Rolf. *Himmelskundliche Ortung auf nordisch-germanischem Boden.* Leipzig: C. Kabitzsch Verlag, 1936.

Mund, Rudolf J. *Der Rasputin Himmlers: Die Wiligut Saga.* Vienna: Volkstum-Verlag, 1982.

Neckel, Gustav and Hans Kuhn. *Edda. Die Lieder des Codex Regius nebst verwandten Denkmälern.* 3d ed. Heidelberg: Winter, 1962.

Osborn, Marijane and Stella Longland. *Rune Games.* London: Routledge and Kegan Paul, 1982.

Pennick, Nigel. *Hitler's Secret Sciences.* Sudbury, Suffolk: Neville Spearman, 1981.

Pushong, Carlyle A. *Rune Magic.* London: Regency, 1978.

Reuter, Sigfrid. *Der Himmel uber den Germanen.* Munich: Zentralverlag der NSDAP, n.d.

Rüsten, Rudolf. *Was tut not? Ein Führer durch die gesamte Literatur der Deutschbewegung.* Leipzig: G. Hedeler, 1914.

Sebottendorf, Rudolf von. *Bevor Hitler kam.* Munich: Deukula Verlag, 1933.

Shou, Peryt [Albert C. G. Schultz]. *Die "Edda" als Schlüssel des kommenden Weltalters!* Vol. 1, *Esoterik der Edda.* Berlin-Pankow: Linser Verlag, [1920].

Spiesberger, Karl. *Runenmagie.* Berlin: Schikowski, 1955.

———. *Runenexerzitien fur Jedermann.* Freiburg/ Breisgau: Bauer, 1958.

———. *Das Mantra Buch.* Berlin: Schikowski, 1977.

Tacitus, Cornelius. *The Agricola and the Germania.* Harmondsworth, UK: Penguin, 1948.

Thorsson, Edred. *The Runic Magic of the Armanen.* Austin, TX: The Rune-Gild, 1980.

———. *Futhark: A Handbook of Rune Magic.* York Beach, ME: Weiser, 1984.

———. *Runelore: A Handbook of Esoteric Runology.* York Beach, ME: Weiser, 1987.

———. *At the Well of Wyrd: A Handbook of Runic Divina-*

tion. York Beach, ME: Weiser, 1988.

Tyson, Donald. *Rune Magic*. St. Paul, MN: Llewellyn Publications, 1988.

Wiligut, Karl Maria [Lobesam, pseud.]. *Seyfrids Runen*. Vienna: F. Schalk, 1903.

Zoller, Robert. *Towards an Esoteric Germanic Astronomy*. Austin, TX: The Rune-Gild, 1984-85.

Periodicals

Hagal. *Ur-Sprache, Ur-Schrift, Ur-Sinn*. Published by the Edda-Gesellschaft. 1934, 1936–1938.

Hag All/All Hag. *Zeitschrift für arische Freiheit*. Verlag Edda-Gesellschaft, Mittenwald, 1933.

Runen. Zeitschrift für germanische Geistesoffenbarungen und Wissenschaften. Merkblatt für den Freundschafts-grad des Germanen-Ordens Walvater. Magdeburg: 1918–1929.

STAY IN TOUCH

On the following pages you will find some of the books now available on related subjects. Your book dealer stocks most of these and will stock new titles in the Llewellyn series as they become available. We urge your patronage.

To obtain our full catalog, to keep informed about new titles as they are released and to benefit from informative articles and helpful news, you are invited to write for our bimonthly news magazine/catalog, *Llewellyn's New Worlds of Mind and Spirit*. A sample copy is free, and it will continue coming to you at no cost as long as you are an active mail customer. Or you may subscribe for just $10.00 in the U.S.A. and Canada ($20.00 overseas, first class mail). Many bookstores also have *New Worlds* available to their customers. Ask for it.

Llewellyn's New Worlds of Mind and Spirit
P.O. Box 64383-778, St. Paul, MN 55164-0383, U.S.A.
* * *

TO ORDER BOOKS AND TAPES

If your book dealer does not have the books described, you may order them directly from the publisher by sending full price in U.S. funds, plus $3.00 for postage and handling for orders *under* $10.00; $4.00 for orders *over* $10.00. There are no postage and handling charges for orders over $50.00. Postage and handling rates are subject to change. We ship UPS whenever possible. Delivery guaranteed. Provide your street address as UPS does not deliver to P.O. Boxes. Allow 4-6 weeks for delivery. UPS to Canada requires a $50.00 minimum order. Orders outside the U.S.A. and Canada: Airmail—add retail price of book; add $5.00 for each non-book item (tapes, etc.); add $1.00 per item for surface mail.

FOR GROUP STUDY AND PURCHASE

Because there is a great deal of interest in group discussion and study of the subject matter of this book, we offer a special quantity price to group leaders or agents. Our special quantity price for a minimum order of five copies of *Rune Might* is $23.85 cash-with-order. This price includes postage and handling within the United States. Minnesota residents must add 6.5% sales tax. For additional quantities, please order in multiples of five. For Canadian and foreign orders, add postage and handling charges as above. Credit card (VISA, MasterCard, American Express) orders are accepted. Charge card orders only ($15.00 minimum order) may be phoned in free within the U.S.A. or Canada by dialing 1-800-THE-MOON. For customer service, call 1-612-291-1970. Mail orders to:

LLEWELLYN PUBLICATIONS
P.O. Box 64383-778, St. Paul, MN 55164-0383, U.S.A.

Prices subject to change without notice.

A BOOK OF TROTH
by Edred Thorsson

One of the most widespread of the ancient pagan revivals is Asatru, or Odinism. Its followers seek to rekindle the way of the North, of the ancient Teutonic peoples. Until now, no book has completely expressed the nature and essence of that movement. *A Book of Troth* is that book.

This is the most traditional and well-informed general guide to the practice of the elder Germanic folk way. The official document of the organization known simply as the "Ring of Troth," *A Book of Troth* is not a holy book or bible in the usual sense. Rather it outlines a code of behavior and a set of actions, not a doctrine or a way of believing.

The first section of the book explores the various important themes or teachings of the religion, laying the intellectual groundwork for the practice. The second section is the heart of the book, since the Troth is a way of doing, not of believing. Here the reader learns how to actually practice the various religious observances with complete rituals, the tools needed, timing, and proper arrangement of the sacred space. The third part of the book outlines the curriculum and training program for qualifying as a priest, priestess or Elder in the Troth.

A Book of Troth presents for the first time the essence of Teutonic neo-paganism between two covers. It is a must for anyone interested in an effective system based on ancient and timeless principles.

0-87542-777-4, 248 pgs., illustrated **$9.95**

RUNE MAGIC
by Donald Tyson

Drawing upon historical records, poetic fragments, and the informed study of scholars, *Rune Magic* resurrects the ancient techniques of this tactile form of magic, and integrates those methods with modern occultism, so that anyone can use the runes in a personal magical system. For the first time, every known and conjectured meaning of all 33 known runes, including the 24 runes known as *futhark*, is available in one volume. In addition, *Rune Magic* covers the use of runes in divination, astral traveling, skrying, and on amulets and talismans. A complete rune ritual is also provided, and 24 rune words are outlined. Gods and Goddesses of the runes are discussed, with illustrations from the National Museum of Sweden.

0-87542-826-6, 210 pgs., 6 x 9, illus., softcover **$9.95**